T0060393

Drop the Rock—
The Ripple Effect

*Using Step Ten to Work Steps
Six and Seven Every Day*

Fred H.

Hazelden
Publishing

Hazelden Publishing
hazelden.org/bookstore

© 2016 by Fred H.
All rights reserved. Published 2016
Printed in the United States of America

No part of this publication, either print or electronic, may be reproduced in any form or by any means without the express written permission of the publisher. Failure to comply with these terms may expose you to legal action and damages for copyright infringement.

ISBN: 978-1-61649-600-5; ebook 978-1-61649-605-0
Library of Congress Cataloging-in-Publication Data is on file at the Library of Congress

Editor's notes

The names, details, and circumstances have been changed to protect the privacy of those mentioned in this publication. See the author's note that follows.

This publication is not intended as a substitute for the advice of health care professionals.

Alcoholics Anonymous, AA, and the Big Book are registered trademarks of Alcoholics Anonymous World Services, Inc.

25 24 23   12 11 10

Developmental editor: Sid Farrar
Production editor: Mindy Keskinen
Interior design and typesetting: Jennifer Dolezal

To my spiritual landscape, Montana, where on clear nights during my childhood the luminous Milky Way gave me glimpses of a Fourth Dimension . . .

To my maternal grandfather, Carl O., whose music, magic, and loving kindness later gave me distant memories of feeling worthy . . .

To my sponsor-in-law, Marion F., who taught us that the only time we needed to meditate and pray and wear the world like a loose garment was now . . . and now . . . and now . . .

And to my wife, Page H., whose life radiates a healing depth of beauty and common sense as we negotiate together our opportunities to grow on the road of happy destiny.

Author's Note

Many of the personal stories in this book are from people I've met in Twelve Step meetings. Others are from participants in recovery workshops and seminars that I've attended or led. A few are from my own life and recovery; some are composites assembled from multiple sources. I've done my best to recall and reconstruct each person's experiences accurately. However, none of these stories is a verbatim transcription. To maintain each person's anonymity, I've changed names and identifying details.

Step Ten

Continued to take personal inventory and when we were wrong promptly admitted it.

Step Six

Were entirely ready to have God remove all these defects of character.

Step Seven

Humbly asked Him to remove our shortcomings.

Contents

Foreword
by William C. Moyers

∞

If you're like me—and my hunch is you are, by your interest in this book—then you reach a point in your recovery where you realize that to stop drinking or taking drugs isn't the hardest part. We did it countless times, didn't we? We learn that our real challenge is to *stay* stopped, because in the end, recovery isn't merely about living life without getting drunk or stoned. It's about living life on life's terms, which can be downright difficult at times.

There are many pathways to overcoming substance use disorders. A well-honed route that works for a lot of us is along the path marked by the Twelve Steps of Alcoholics Anonymous. It is a program of recovery that begins with Step One, where we acknowledge the omnipotence of alcohol and other drugs, their ability to hijack our brains and steal our souls, and our inability to overcome the problem using our own free will alone. Yet it is only in this first Step that the specific substance—whether it's alcohol, opiates, marijuana, or another addictive drug—is explicitly called out as part of the problem. The remaining Steps make no mention of the substance itself, because on this pathway to recovery the substance is but a symptom; the addiction is a sickness of not only the body but the mind and spirit as well.

And the solution is a new way of life provided by working these remaining Steps. Abstinence is a necessary goal, for sure, but recovery is much more than abstinence—it demands wholesale transformation.

For too long a time I didn't grasp this fact. And so after every hangover, every consequence, and every regret I vowed to quit, again and again and again. And always I picked up again. Until one day a long time ago when I finally understood that what needed to change was far more than my harmful use of addictive substances. At last I accepted that *I* needed to change, from the inside out, and I've been a work in progress ever since.

That's why this little book is so important. In recovery, for the newcomer and veteran alike, it is our own thoughts and behaviors that demand ongoing vigilance. Our character flaws, sharp edges, and shortcomings are as toxic and damaging to ourselves and the people in our lives as the substances once were to our bodies. When we stop using, these flaws don't simply disappear. There they are, to be recognized, confronted, and then neutralized, if not outright removed—and not just by ourselves alone. Our effort requires the help of others, including our Higher Power. This remains true as the days turn to months, the months to years, and the years to our lifetime of commitment to staying well. This is the power of Step Ten, to remind us that we only have to turn to that help one day at a time; when we do, the lifetime will take care of itself.

Even the fleetest marathon runner still must cover the distance one stride at a time. And yet the irritation from the smallest pebble in a shoe can soon fester into a painful blister as debilitating as a heavy stone carried over a shoulder, imperiling one's ability to finish the race at all. So it is in recovery. Our pebble may be a little white lie, a selfish act nobody else notices, the silent resentment harbored towards a colleague's success, a minor run-in with the law, or a hurtful rant fueled by fear-ignited anger. These are just a few of the countless ways the shortcomings of our imperfect humanness can show themselves. Sure, we've stopped drinking and taking drugs. But to go on living and growing requires that we free ourselves daily of the weight of these imperfections. Even with the success we found in working the first nine Steps, we may discover that now, further along our recovery journey, we've again picked up some of the weight we thought we had dropped and left behind. When this happens, "progress, not perfection" has never sounded so good. ("I'm sorry" resonates, too, when called for.) Step Ten reminds us that progress is our goal. By removing the "pebbles" along the way, we can release those weights before they become too great to bear.

Addiction is an illness of isolation, shame, and hopelessness. Its antidote includes what the reader will find in the pages that follow. This book reminds us that our journey requires the diligence of steady effort to "grow in understanding and effectiveness," as the Big Book puts it, so that we may enjoy our place in "the world of the Spirit."

Onward we go, together.

William Cope Moyers
Author of *Now What? An Insider's Guide to Addiction and Recovery* and *Broken: My Story of Addiction and Redemption*

Welcome to the Voyage of Recovery

∞

You may be familiar with some version of the Drop the Rock parable. It's about the Twelve Step group members who set sail on the ship *Recovery* across the sea of Life for the island of Serenity. As the parable is usually told, soon after the boat pulls away from the dock, the passengers realize that some of their friends are not yet on board.

Sure enough, their friend Mary comes running down the street and onto the dock. The people on the boat cheer her on. "Dive in and swim, Mary!" they shout. "You can do it!" Mary dives into the water and swims for the boat as fast and hard as she can. But as she gets close to the boat, she slows and struggles to stay afloat. Everyone on board can see why: a heavy rock is hanging from a snarl of strings around Mary's neck. "Drop the rock!" they all shout. "Let go! Drop the rock!"

Treading water, Mary looks down at the rock. She realizes it contains her fear, resentments, self-pity, anger, intolerance, resentments, and other character flaws. She also realizes that if she doesn't let go of them, she will drown.

She tears off the strings, holds the rock away from her body, and lets it go.

Freed of the heavy and useless weight, Mary easily swims the rest of the way to the boat. She climbs aboard, dripping and deeply relieved.

When most people tell this story, this is where they stop. That's understandable, because that part alone is useful and instructive.

But here's how that parable might continue: As Mary is drying off, she notices something heavy in her pants pocket. She reaches in and discovers another rock, although much smaller than the one she'd just released. She recognizes this as her character defect of self-centeredness and immediately tosses it into the water.

As everyone congratulates Mary, they look back toward shore. Someone else is in the water, swimming desperately toward the boat. But that person, too, is being pulled underwater after every few strokes.

As the swimmer gets closer to the boat, Mary can see that it's Ramon, her old friend and—before they went through treatment together—drinking buddy.

Mary runs to the rail, leans over, and shouts, "Hey, Ramon, it's me, Mary! Drop the rock! Can you see the ripples from the rocks I just dropped? We don't have to carry around our character defects any more. If I can do it, you can!"

As the ripples from Mary's rocks reach Ramon, he pulls the strings off his shoulders and raises his hand above his head in a thumbs-up.

"You're almost there!" Mary shouts.

"I'm coming!" Ramon shouts back.

He dives under the ripples and disappears. Half a minute later, his head pops out of the water, only thirty feet from the boat.

He disappears beneath the water again. Everyone on board watches breathlessly.

Then suddenly Ramon appears next to the boat, just below Mary. He gasps, "Help me in!"

Mary leans over, stretches out her arm, and pulls Ramon aboard.

Welcome Aboard

This book is for anyone on a journey of recovery. It's anchored in the Twelve Steps and Twelve Traditions of Alcoholics Anonymous—principles that can be applied to all kinds of recovery. (These Twelve Steps and Twelve Traditions appear in full at the back of this book.)

Drop the Rock—The Ripple Effect focuses specifically on Steps Six, Seven, and Ten:

- *Step Six:* Were entirely ready to have God remove all our defects of character.

- *Step Seven:* Humbly asked God to remove our shortcomings.

- *Step Ten:* Continued to take personal inventory and when we were wrong promptly admitted it.

In some ways, this book is a follow-up to *Drop the Rock: Removing Character Defects.* Written by recovery veterans Bill P., Todd W., and Sara S., that groundbreaking book helped unpack the power and potential of Steps Six and Seven. And it spoke to a real need, because those two Steps are only briefly discussed in the book *Alcoholics Anonymous*—commonly called the Big Book—which serves as a basic text for many in recovery. In fact, the Big Book devotes only two paragraphs to these Steps, which leaves a lot of people looking for guidance on how to actually put them into action in their lives. Even the dozen pages devoted to Steps Six and Seven in *Twelve Steps and Twelve Traditions* often get lost in the shuffle, as too many people today either don't read or only skim this important book. When *Drop the Rock: Removing Character Defects* was first published in 1993, it was the only book to fill this long-overlooked gap. Since then, hundreds of thousands of people in recovery have found that book immensely valuable.

If you've already read *Drop the Rock: Removing Character Defects,* congratulations! If you haven't, I recommend that you pick up a copy and read it. It will add depth, perspective, and a new dimension to your practice of Steps Six and Seven. But even if you haven't read that book, no worries. Anyone working a Twelve Step program can get a great deal out of *Drop the Rock— The Ripple Effect.*

What makes each of these two books unique?

Drop the Rock: Removing Character Defects is especially helpful for people who are working (or about to work) Steps Six and Seven for the first time. It's also of great value for people who thought they had been working these Steps, but have realized that they were only going through the motions. They hadn't yet made the all-important turn of humbly and honestly asking to be transformed—in very specific, uniquely personal ways—by a Higher Power.

Drop the Rock—The Ripple Effect is particularly valuable for folks who have *already* worked all the preparation Steps (One through Three) and all the action Steps (Four through Nine). Now they have begun to work the maintenance Steps. These people are no longer learning how to work the Program. They are learning how to make the Program a way of life, day by day and moment by moment. They are also shifting from a focus on self to a focus on service.

If this describes you, then please accept my special welcome aboard. In this book, it's my goal to offer you guidance, tips, and insights—as well as many simple, practical exercises for working Steps Six and Seven in the course of working Step Ten. You'll also read stories of a variety folks in recovery who have used Step Ten as a compass for navigating Steps Six and Seven.

The Ripple Effect

What is the Ripple Effect? *It's the effect we have on other human beings*, based on what we do (or don't do), what we say (or don't say), and how we show up in each moment in other people's lives.

When we act from one of our shortcomings or character defects—impatience, let's say—we don't just harm ourselves. We send ripples of negativity out to the people around us.

For example, your decision to cut in front of another driver on the highway may result in that person getting angry or anxious. It may also cause a collision. That collision, in turn, may make the driver late for an important job interview. And, because she doesn't get that job, she and her partner can't afford to pay their medical bills. Six months later, they are forced to file for bankruptcy. This may be an extreme example, but it demonstrates how seemingly inconsequential actions can have dramatic effects.

In contrast, when we follow the spiritual guidance of the Twelve Steps and a Higher Power, acting from a spirit of service, what we do (or don't do) ripples out to the people around us as well—but in a positive way. Instead of letting ourselves be pushed around by our impatience, we recognize *in that moment* that it has risen up inside us. In the next moment, we identify it as a shortcoming. In the next, we recognize that we—and the world—would be better off if we didn't act from that impatience. And in the next, we ask our Higher Power to take our impatience from us.

This very process has transformed us, in that short string of moments, from impatient to patient.

Imagine that this transformation happens to you on the road to work. Instead of cutting off the driver in the next lane, you smile and wave her in front of you.

She smiles and waves back.

An hour later, she aces her interview. A week later, she gets the job. Although neither of you realizes it, four years later she hires you as her assistant. She turns out to be the best boss you've ever had.

When most of us first begin working Step Ten, we take a nightly personal inventory. We acknowledge the character flaws we recognized that day and ask our Higher Power to remove them.

Over time, this daily practice can evolve into one that we do several times each day. Eventually we do it in *the very moment* when we catch ourselves acting out of one of our shortcomings or character defects. As we keep working Step Ten, we learn to catch ourselves even sooner—whenever we have the *impulse* to act from one of our character flaws. With practice, we then learn to be aware of the rising of an emotion that generates or precedes such an impulse.

Then, one day, we discover that working Step Ten in each moment has become as natural to us as walking, or dressing, or chatting with friends.

A Few Words about God and Higher Power

In this book I use a variety of terms to describe the spiritual nature of Twelve Step recovery, as does each of the storytellers. When you read these terms—Higher Power, Power greater than ourselves, God as I understand God, Him, Creator, and so on— please substitute any concept that keeps what some have called "the power of possibility" open for you.

The source of this suggestion is the Big Book: "When, therefore, we use the word God, we mean your own conception of God. This applies, too, to *other spiritual expressions* which you find in this book" (page 47, lines 1–3). (All Big Book citations in these pages refer to the fourth edition of *Alcoholics Anonymous*, published in 2002.)

Some of us walked away from religion a long time ago and aren't the least bit interested in going down that road again. Even when we experienced the friendliness and understanding showered on us in the rooms as newcomers, it was hard not to be suspicious that there was religion in there somewhere too. Thank *goodness* (one of my favorite spiritual expressions) we can find a way to tolerate the language we find off-putting as we continue to seek Twelve Step help until that time when we actually experience the obstacles in our lives beginning to melt away. At that point, having had our own spiritual awakening, we can see that these terms are just many names for what we have found through working the Steps.

So use the term or terms that are comfortable for you. Just as no one can work the Steps for you, no one can have a spiritual experience on your behalf. Our own stories of suffering, getting sober, and joyfully living clean and sober are as personal as our own DNA.

The Twelve Steps as a Sequence

∞

The Big Book doesn't teach us hundreds of different things; it teaches us a small number of things hundreds of times. And those few things are presented in a sequence.

When most of us began working the Steps, we saw them as simply a list, much like the Ten Commandments. Now, however, we understand that the *specific sequence of the Twelve Steps is the transformative element of the Program.* The Twelve Steps are a unified, interdependent whole, not a collection of twelve separate items. Each Step requires and builds on *all* of the earlier Steps.

As the Big Book explains on page xxii, the Twelve Steps *trace exactly the same path to recovery that was blazed by the earliest members of Alcoholics Anonymous.* That paragraph also makes clear that *The Twelve Steps . . . summarize the program.*

Step One is the truth about the problem: it gets our attention and gives meaning to our struggle. Step Two is the truth about the solution, based on the truth about the problem. Step Three is the truth about what blocks us from experiencing a solution. Steps Four through Nine get us unblocked. Steps Ten through Twelve *keep* us unblocked. Or, to put it another way: Step One is where we were. Step Two is where we wanted to be. Steps Three through Nine are how we get well. And Steps Ten through Twelve are how we stay well.

As old-timers Joe and Charlie pointed out in their workshops and in their book *A Program for You,* the Big Book is organized in a very deliberate sequence. Because it is a textbook for recovery, it is meant to be read and studied in that sequence. And that sequence begins this way: *We have a problem. The problem defines the solution. And there are prescribed actions that can bring about a solution.*

Most of us in recovery know a number of Twelve Step slogans, such as "First Things First," "Easy Does It," and "It Works if You Work It." Each of these can be helpful and inspiring at various points in our recovery. But we get the most benefit from them as guideposts to a new way of life in the context of this simple three-part template of *problem, solution, and program of action provided by the Twelve Steps.*

If we practice each of the Steps as an individual strategy, they may give us some benefit and relief. But for them to become an unshakable foundation for living, the Steps must be practiced in the order in which they were written and *lived into* over a lifetime.

The Twelve Steps as Activities

The word *step* is both a verb and a noun.

When most of us think of the word, we tend to envision a step on a staircase—a static object that helps us move upward and forward. But the Twelve Steps are neither static nor objects. A *step* is also an action that can be performed by the body and the mind. This definition best embodies the Twelve Steps. They are *living* steps—as well as steps for living.

A list of the Twelve Steps, as they appear in the Big Book, hangs on the wall at most recovery group meetings. But these words themselves aren't the Steps; they're a summary of the Steps. We don't work the Steps by reciting them, discussing them, and reflecting on them. *We work the Steps by practicing them in all our affairs,* as Step Twelve reminds us.

When a Twelve Step meeting focuses on Step Six, Seven, or both, the meeting tends to be short. People generally don't have much to say about those Steps, perhaps because of the Big Book's lack of concrete direction about them, as noted earlier.

As a result, many of us in recovery don't actually work Steps Six and Seven—some call them the *drive-by Steps*. Instead, we recite them, discuss them, study them, and reflect on them. *We practice the summaries on the wall instead of the Steps themselves.*

This was certainly true in my case. I was sober for twelve years before I saw the difference between the Steps on the wall and the deeply human activity of working them.

The Steps on the wall are only the Cliffs Notes version of the Twelve Steps. Back in high school, if you had read the Cliffs Notes for *The Great Gatsby* but not the actual novel, you probably would have been able to pass a multiple-choice test on the book. You might even have been able to discuss it fairly intelligently. But you wouldn't have actually *experienced* the novel. You'd have missed its essence—as well as the pleasure of experiencing all the events in it and the development of the characters as they unfolded.

Jerry: I was practicing the "wall Steps"

When I lived in Manhattan, I went to a lot of AA meetings in the city, in Connecticut, and in New Jersey. I won't say I was unhappy in my sobriety—it saved my life and my career—but I didn't find the meetings that fulfilling. After three years of sobriety and recovery, the Twelve Step meetings started seeming familiar and repetitive. To me they were like trips to the dentist—necessary and healthy, but not anything I enjoyed or looked forward to.

I was kind of puzzled by how, in meetings, some people would glow like they were at a religious revival. At that point in my recovery, I'd never felt anything like that. The Twelve Steps made sense to me, and they'd made a big difference in my life, but they never revved me up or made energy rush up my spine.

I assumed I must have had a spiritual awakening somewhere along the way, because I was sober, I hadn't relapsed in almost two years, and I was feeling okay. But I'd never had a mind-blowing, omigod experience.

One day I went to a meeting in Maine while I was visiting the state. There a woman told her story about how she'd changed when she shifted from the wall Steps to the actual Steps. I'd never heard that distinction before, or even heard the term *wall Steps*.

Afterward I asked her to explain it to me in more detail. That's when she told me about the Twelve Steps as a sequence and a process, and how the Steps on the wall are just a summary of that process. Then she said, "You can't live a summary."

I hadn't heard the Steps described that way before and was stunned. The next night, I started rereading the Big Book from the beginning, this time being much more careful and thorough. From then on, each day I'd read four or five pages and examine them carefully in my mind. This time through, something about the Big Book felt different. Something about me felt different too.

After about four months of doing this, I had a vital spiritual experience: the kind that so many people in the Program talk about. It wasn't a profound revelation that made my jaw drop or my hair stand on end. It was almost the opposite. It was a deep sense of peace and relief—one that stayed with me and is with me still. I can feel it throughout my body.

Then a few weeks after that, a totally unexpected thing happened. Even though I'd had a spiritual awakening—in fact, *because* I'd had a spiritual awakening—I started to feel resentment toward all the groups I'd gone to during those first three years of my recovery.

In all that time, in half a dozen groups, and two or three hundred meetings, they'd let me get away with doing the wall Steps, especially when it came to Steps Six and Seven.

For a few weeks, this resentment grew inside me. It got to where I'd go to a meeting and spend half the time being angry at the very people who were there to support me. And I was angry at *them* for not adequately supporting me!

After about a month, I realized that my resentment had become a real problem. I needed to be restored to sanity. I called my sponsor, Nate, and said, "I'm in trouble."

The next morning we had breakfast, and I told him what I was feeling. It sounded bizarre, even to me. I'd had a spiritual awakening, and I was resenting Twelve Step groups because I hadn't had that awakening sooner.

Nate listened thoughtfully as I talked. When I was done, all he said was, "So Jerry, what character defect or shortcoming do you think is behind your resentment?"

His comment was so on the money that it made me laugh. My spiritual awakening was absolutely, completely real. But there was still a part of me that hadn't gotten well, and now it was rearing its head. Part of me still needed to resent something. I was actually jealous of people in other groups who had received spiritual awakenings sooner than I did. As if we were somehow in competition.

Nate encouraged me to work Step Ten right there at the breakfast table—which of course meant working Steps Four through Nine first.

As we finished our coffee, I was able to admit the nature of my resentment. Then I said softly to my Higher Power, "Please take this resentment away." A moment later, our waiter appeared, gestured toward our plates, and asked, "Shall I take these away for you?" I thought, *Good timing.*

My resentment wasn't whisked away as quickly as our plates were. But I left our breakfast feeling much lighter. And over the next few days, I felt the resentment slowly leaving me, like a wound steadily healing.

Now let's take a closer look at Steps Six and Seven and the transformation they can continue to bring about in our lives through working Step Ten.

The Transformation of
Steps Six and Seven

E ven though Steps Six and Seven are sometimes called the forgotten Steps because so little has been written about them, they may be among the most crucial of all the Twelve Steps. When we work them—or, more accurately, when we let them work on us—we make a fundamental and all-important change. *We move from a reliance on self-direction to a reliance on spiritual direction.*

In working these Steps, we admit that we can't recover on our own; we have to ask for help from a Higher Power. And we don't ask for this help in a way that suggests we don't have to change. Instead we say, *I know I'm going to have to change, and I can't do that on my own—I need a power greater than self to make that happen.*

As many people discover, this transformation isn't something that happens only to those of us in recovery. It is one of the most crucial actions *any* human being can take to live a truly meaningful life: a life of service.

When many of us worked Steps Six and Seven for the first time, we felt great relief and release. We let go of a great burden that had weighed us down for years. We crossed a threshold that led to hope and healing—and the possibility of a new life.

Then Steps Eight and Nine helped us move into that new life by removing the weight of our harms to others and bringing us to the realization that our Higher Power "is doing for us what we could not do for ourselves." Now, as we work Step Ten, we see that it makes our new life sustainable. Step Ten is the *ongoing* practice of Steps Four through Nine, with an emphasis on Six and Seven.

Step Ten: Not a Threshold, but a Way of Being

Steps Six and Seven are at the numerical center of the Twelve Steps. The first six focus on the past, while the commitment we make to allow change in Step Seven begins to move us forward on the Road of Happy Destiny.

Steps Six and Seven also form the fulcrum of the core action steps, Four though Nine. They enable us to shift from what *was* to what *will be.*

The Big Book's two paragraphs on these Steps refer to two key elements: an essential attitude, *willingness,* and the time frame for living into that attitude: *now.*

But *now* is not a one-time event. The time is *always* now. Think of Step Ten: "Continued to take personal inventory and when we were wrong promptly admitted it." That means willingly practicing Steps Four through Nine again and again, moment by moment, one day at a time.

As part of Step Ten, we do regular moral inventories—as well as an on-the-spot inventory whenever we feel we might have harmed someone. If we have in fact caused harm, we make things right with the affected people, with our Higher Power, and with ourselves as soon as we can.

I've already mentioned Joe and Charlie, the old-timers who led highly regarded Big Book workshops across the country for many years and who published a book version of those workshops, *A Program for You.* They had a tremendous influence on my understanding of the Big Book—especially regarding the importance of working the Steps *in order.* Joe and Charlie suggest that we view Step Six as a guide to no longer doing what we want to do, and Step Seven as a guide to doing what we don't (yet) want to do, but know we need to. Or to put it another way, in

Step Six we abandon what's no longer of use to us; in Step Seven we vow to do what *will* be useful to us and others.

Now, as we work Step Ten, we stop caring so much about what we want and don't want to do. We drop our focus on ourselves and make an ongoing commitment to do what is sane and loving and responsible, over and over. We focus on being fully present and preparing for a life of service that we commit to in Step Twelve. We bring the spiritual essence of the Program, which is embodied in Steps Six and Seven, to each circumstance we encounter.

Step Ten provides a doorway—a new dimension—for working Steps Six and Seven more deeply and profoundly. Over time, we discover that Step Ten is the key to long-term sobriety.

Bonita: Working Step Ten on the way to Reno

I was a serious meth user for several years in my teens. Fortunately, by age seventeen I knew I had to choose between sobriety and an early death. I started going to meetings in eleventh grade, and I've been clean and sober now for more than eight years. I've got a wonderful partner and a great career, and I'm endlessly grateful to the Program, my sponsors, and all the others who have helped and supported me.

My job involves a lot of traveling. A few months ago, for the first time, I had to drive through Nevada. I stopped for lunch at a hotel restaurant in Reno, and afterward I put about ten bucks into the slots and won 180 dollars. I thought, *Great. That will cover lunch and the next payment on my college loan.*

Two days later, driving back home, I stopped for dinner at the same hotel. Afterward, I did the same thing—put about fifteen dollars into the slots. And again I won—about 90 bucks. It felt good.

A few weeks later, I had to make the same trip again. By the time I crossed the Nevada state line, I was thinking about stopping at the same hotel and playing the slots again. I noticed that I was feeling some serious excitement and euphoria and anticipation.

I shook it off and played some tunes on my phone. But the fantasy of pulling the handle and winning big returned. Only this time I got so lost in it that I almost sideswiped somebody in the next lane. That's when I knew it was time for a Step Ten.

I looked at the driver in the next lane, who was giving me the finger. I mouthed "I'm sorry" and slapped my head. He nodded, put his hand down, and pulled away.

I stopped at the next roadside restaurant. I sat down with a coffee and silently prayed for help. Even though I'd never had an issue with gambling before—the most I'd done was buy a lottery ticket now and then—I knew I was in trouble.

The solution came to me before I finished my coffee. I bought a sandwich to go, ate it in the car an hour later, and drove straight through Reno and across the Nevada border, stopping only to use the ladies' room.

The everyday practice of Step Ten is clearly described on page 84 of the Big Book: *Continue to watch for selfishness, dishonesty, resentment and fear* (Step Four). *When these crop up, we ask God at once to remove them* (Steps Six and Seven). Those last eight words contain the essence of Steps Six and Seven.

The directions for Step Ten continue, *We share them with someone immediately* (Step Five) *and make amends quickly if we have harmed anyone* (Steps Eight and Nine). Thus, in just a few sentences, the Big Book's Step Ten directions clearly lay out the practices of Steps Four through Nine—now applied to what arises in the moment, and to the conditions of everyday life.

As we live according to the wisdom of Step Ten, we continue to spot and respond to our wrongs, shortcomings, and character defects. Over time, we tend to spot ever-smaller ones—partly because we have now addressed the larger ones, partly because we've become more attuned to spotting things as they pop up. We see things that we might not even have called wrongs or shortcomings or character defects a few years ago. *Once we've gotten rid of the biggest rocks, we can begin to see and feel the smaller ones.*

In the story about Mary and Ramon, each swimmer drops a single large rock and immediately begins to lead a less burdened life. That's an accurate description of most people's first Step Six and Step Seven. But many of us feel like we need to keep dropping rocks every day. And they're not always little rocks—sometimes they're huge. On some days, we have to drop multiple rocks. And sometimes the rock we dropped days or months or years ago shows up again, and we have to drop it once more—in some cases, multiple times.

That's why Step Ten is so helpful—and so vital.

Larry: Momentum lost can be regained

Last year I fulfilled a dream I've had since I was a boy—I began singing in an Anglican choir. For eight months, it was one of the most fulfilling things I'd ever done.

I live out in the country, and my church is in the city, about forty-five miles away. This meant driving ninety miles on Wednesday nights and Saturday afternoons for rehearsals—and, of course, on Sunday mornings and high holidays.

I've been in recovery over eleven years. I know that I'm still powerless over alcohol, but I no longer want to drink. Alcohol and a self-centered life nearly destroyed me and my family. I go to two meetings a week and haven't missed one in years.

But I did miss a Wednesday night choir rehearsal. I came down with a stomach bug, so I called the choir director and she agreed that the best thing was for me to stay home.

I went to Saturday rehearsal as usual, but on Sunday our car didn't start, so I missed church. Then, three days later, our water heater sprang a serious leak a few minutes before it was time to leave for the city. By the time I had everything cleaned up, I knew I'd arrive shortly before rehearsal ended, so I stayed home.

After that, my momentum was gone. When Saturday morning came, I was surprisingly resistant. All I could think about was the ninety-mile trip and how long and tedious it would be. I *really* didn't want to go—even though I still really enjoyed singing. I found myself thinking, *Maybe I should quit the choir.*

Something about that thought made me stop and examine it. Its tone was vaguely familiar. After a minute or two, I recognized the voice. It was a voice I hadn't heard in years. It was the voice that had said, early in my recovery, *Maybe you should quit the Program. Go have a drink instead.*

That's when I realized that sustained momentum is part of what drives recovery. And Step Ten is partly about sustaining momentum. I threw myself into the car and started driving to church.

I made sure to get to every one of the next several rehearsals, and kept checking myself daily to see if my momentum had returned. It took a few weeks, but eventually it did.

I thank God that, over the last eleven years, I never lost my momentum in going to meetings or practicing the Steps.

—————————————

When we first practiced Steps Six and Seven wholeheartedly, they transformed us.

Step Six followed us from our past. It helped us to honestly see our limitations and our humanness. It enabled us look at where we didn't want to go—but knew we needed to.

Step Seven led us into the future, into a new way of being in the world. It shifted our perspective from our rear view mirror to the open road before us.

Step Ten uses Steps Six and Seven to ground us in the present—where our human-ness and our being-ness come together.

As we practice Step Ten, day by day and moment by moment, it continuously transforms us and all our relationships. We move from establishing a relationship with our Higher Power to experiencing that Power in all our relationships. We move from hearing each Step resonate in our head to feeling it in our guts, bones, and blood. We move from *learning* the Steps to *living* them.

Most of all, we move from a focus on our own growth and transformation to a focus on how our behavior affects others. This change in focus is what I call the Ripple Effect.

As We Cross the Sea of Life

∞◇∞

As beloved AA speaker Chuck C. has observed, when we first began working the Program, we thought that alcohol (or drugs, or overeating, or whatever) was our problem, because we have a body that can't tolerate it, coupled with a mind that can't leave it alone.

But when we first used alcohol, it wasn't a problem for us—it was an answer. That's why we drank—or shot up, or overate, or gambled away our savings. This means that our foundational problem existed before we began drinking or drugging or overeating.

By the time we reach Step Ten, we clearly understand what that foundational problem is: *overreliance on self.* That was our single biggest character defect, and for much or our life, it blocked us from having a spiritual experience.

I smile when I hear people refer to the Twelve Steps as a self-help program, because it's exactly the opposite. Our "selves" need help. *The Twelve Steps teach us how and when to ask for help from a Higher Power*—not how to rely more on the self and self-centeredness.

When we reach Step Ten, we are no longer drinking or using or overeating. But something much greater has also occurred: we've sobered up to our humanness—to our limitations. We've also sobered up to our need to grow and serve on an ongoing basis. We know that we cannot simply settle for chemical relief. We know that if chemical relief is all we focus on, we have taken the first step toward relapse.

As we work Step Ten, we also come to understand some subtle aspects of the Program that are not generally visible to newcomers. Our attitude toward the Steps has shifted—and continues to shift—in profound ways. Let's look closely at some of these shifts.

From Dependence to Service, and from Domination to Assertiveness

As we work Step Ten and it becomes integrated into our life, we let go of trying to control the world—or other people.

We see that our former strategies of demanding, dominating, manipulating, wheedling, flattering, and people pleasing were all forms of overreliance on self. We also come to see that these strategies were the source of most of our (and anyone's) defective interactions.

Now, as we practice Step Ten, we stop looking to others to fulfill us. Instead, we focus on how we can be of service—while also noticing and acknowledging our own needs.

Being of service doesn't mean becoming a doormat. It's exactly the opposite. We learn to become assertive instead of aggressive or dependent. Instead of trying to get others to do what we want, we do whatever is compassionate, or just, or most appropriate for the situation.

We also speak the truth about who we are and what we're feeling. We learn what our real needs are, and we learn to express them clearly and directly, without trying to manipulate others into fulfilling them. We understand that assertiveness is our perfect right—as well as the antidote to the demands we used to make of others.

We are also aware that we can never know exactly how others will respond. When we express ourselves and our needs clearly and directly, they might happily accommodate us. Or they might say "Not gonna happen" or "Not interested" or "Screw you for asking" or even "Screw you for needing that."

Throughout my drinking years and during the first few years of my recovery, I was a compulsive people pleaser. I would do whatever I felt would make others happy and comfortable, in the hope that they would think favorably of me. This was one of my biggest character defects. It was also a subtle form of domination, because I was trying to get everybody else to do my bidding. Through my people pleasing, I demanded that others meet a need in me, which was to be liked. *I was focused on myself, and I compulsively tried to get others to focus on me as well.*

Bill W. had the very same character defect. In his 1958 *Grapevine* article "The Next Frontier: Emotional Sobriety," he observed that his own painful dependencies caused him to demand that other people in AA meet his needs. Repeatedly, he tried to get others to do his bidding and depend upon him. Eventually he recognized that he lacked *emotional sobriety.* From an emotional standpoint, he was still acting like an addict.

During those years when I too lacked emotional sobriety, I radiated an essence of neediness and unsteadiness that blocked me from having a spiritual experience. Now imagine the essence you radiate when you simply show up as yourself in a spirit of compassion and service, and let other people know exactly who you are and what you feel.

Over time, as we work Step Ten, one of the things that changes is the essence of what we radiate. Some people call it a vibe or an intangible influence. This is the energy behind the Ripple Effect.

Discerning Character Defects and Shortcomings

In his preface to *Drop the Rock: Removing Character Defects,* Bill P. wrote:

During the early 1980s I worked in the archives at AA Headquarters in New York and one of the most asked questions was, "What is the difference between character defects and shortcomings?" The answer is that there is no difference. Bill W. and the authors of the Big Book didn't want to use the same word in both Steps. The same approach is used in this book—"character defects" is used interchangeably with "shortcomings."

When we work Steps Six and Seven for the first time, there truly is no difference between the two. We ask God to take away everything that blocks us, holds us back, or keeps us locked inside the grip of self. We don't analyze which of those things are too big or too small, too strong or too weak.

And we don't need to. If we're giving away a bunch of old clothes that no longer fit us, we don't need to separate them into those that are too small because they shrank and those that are too big because we lost weight. We just place everything together in the same bag.

Now that we are working Step Ten, however, we begin to see some subtleties that weren't visible earlier in our recovery. In long-term sobriety, we are able to take a finer measurement of our flaws.

For starters, we begin to realize that most shortcomings and character defects aren't aspects of our personality that are inherently wrong or bad, and therefore need to be destroyed. They are normal human emotions, impulses, and actions that are *over-expressed* or *under-expressed*.

We can call our flaws of under-expression our shortcomings, because they fall short of healthy and compassionate behavior. And we can call our flaws of over-expression our character defects. Or, to borrow a phrase from *Twelve Steps and Twelve Traditions*, our character defects are normal, healthy things that exceed their proper functions, while our shortcomings are normal, healthy things that aren't reaching their minimal levels of effectiveness.

For example, the impulse to speak is normal and healthy. But if I routinely talk too much, or too often, or too loudly, that's a character defect—an over-expression of that impulse. And if I don't speak up when I witness abuse or evil, that's a short-coming—an under-expression of that same normal impulse.

This viewpoint has profound implications for how we see ourselves and our recovery. We're not—and never were—bad people who needed to become good. We're good people who needed to get well—*and who now need to stay well.*

Our shortcomings and character defects are our hardwired human traits and instincts that need to be adjusted up or down, day by day, through the process of recovery. In working Step Ten, we can begin to discern which of our flaws involve the over-expression of these traits, and which ones involve their under-expression.

One example is fear. For our survival and well-being, we all need to be afraid—but only when there's something worth fear-ing. If we're afraid when there's nothing to be afraid of, that is surely a character defect. And if we feel no fear in the face of genuine physical danger, that is clearly a shortcoming.

Here's another example: when we first began working the Steps, some of us had too little self-esteem—an under-expression of a healthy, humble sense of self. Some of us had too much self-esteem—an over-expression of that same basic trait. Some of us suffered from *both* flaws.

As we work Step Ten, part of our responsibility is to be as alert as we can to any overdevelopment or underdevelopment. Then we do what we can to bring that character trait back into balance. We do this by working Steps Six and Seven—and, if appropriate, the five-Step sequence of Five through Nine—as soon as possible after sensing that imbalance. We recognize and name each flaw, and then ask our Higher Power to remove it from us.

If we do at least one thing each day to achieve better balances, then we are on the path of a balanced life. And when we discover that we can't restore balance on our own, we ask our Higher Power to restore it for us by removing the shortcoming or character defect that unbalanced us.

When we first worked Step Four, making our first searching and fearless moral inventory of ourselves, we did so carefully, deliberately, and methodically. In Step Ten this process becomes more fluid and spontaneous. We have developed the discernment for spotting and identifying our character flaws. We've put in place an internal sensor that lights up when a shortcoming or character defect has appeared. We then use the information from this sensor to take personal inventory as soon as possible.

The Big Book summarizes this process on page 84, suggesting that we "continue to watch for selfishness, dishonesty, resentment, and fear." This is the Step Ten version of Step Four.

It's important to draw a distinction between a flaw and the emotion associated with that flaw. In the above passage, selfishness and dishonesty are clearly flaws. (Selfishness is a character defect: an overdeveloped sense of self-interest. Dishonesty, too, is a shortcoming: an underdeveloped sense of truthfulness.) But resentment and fear aren't flaws; they're the primary emotions typically *associated with* selfishness and dishonesty.

This is a crucial insight, because *the emotion we feel often points to the shortcoming or character defect that gives rise to it.* So when our internal sensor picks up resentment and fear, those feelings guide us to look for the selfishness and dishonesty behind them.

The opposite is true as well. When our internal sensor tells us that selfishness or dishonesty has shown up, we learn to look for resentment and fear, knowing there's a good chance we'll find them.

One last thought on this subject: *Every human being shares the same foundational character defect: an overreliance on self.* This is the deeper truth of Step Three, which requires us—not once, but time and time again—to turn our will and our life over to the care of the God of our understanding.

In working Step Ten, we learn from experience that over-reliance on self will manifest over and over, in a nearly infinite variety of forms, guises, and situations. And when we see that happening, we also learn to address it by working Steps Six and Seven as soon as we can.

Sustainable and Unsustainable Emotions

As part of working Step Ten, we learn to pay attention to our emotions as they arise in each new moment.

When used properly, our emotions help us stay alive and healthy. Fear keeps us safe. Guilt prevents us from repeating a harmful action. Awe keeps us humble and grateful. In a balanced life, our emotions serve as valuable and faithful indicators of how we're living and how we're using our free will. They often also point to what we're planning to do next—and, sometimes, to what we need to do instead.

Before we began working the Steps, we viewed our emotions as a posse of friends and a group of enemies. Our life consisted mostly of wanting to experience pleasant emotions and avoid unpleasant ones.

Now, however, we realize that this was a hallmark of our lack of emotional sobriety. We also understand that simply trying to feel good is a road that leads to relapse. In working Step Ten, we let go of the distinction of *pleasant* and *unpleasant*, and instead we focus on whether an emotion points toward a *sustainable* or *unsustainable* recovery and life.

The emotions that point us toward a sustainable life are themselves sustainable. No matter how much of them we experience, they continue to support our lives. Sustainable emotions include peace of mind, connectedness, love, compassion, joy, serenity, and peace.

The emotions that lead us toward an unsustainable life are themselves inherently unsustainable. The more they grow, the more they can get in the way. The most common unsustainable emotions are the unpleasant ones: shame, guilt, remorse, resentment, anger, rage, irritability, and so on. Quite a few are forms of fear, such as anxiety, unease, panic, and terror. When we feel these emotions briefly, we pay attention to them, identify their source and whether they're cues to some action we need to take to regain balance in our lives, and then we let them go. Treated this way, they're not a problem. However, if we cling to them and keep feeding them, eventually they will harm us—and, often, allow us to harm others.

But there's another group of emotions that are equally unsustainable—yet they feel pleasant, at least at first. These include arrogance, overconfidence, excessive pride, superiority, self-righteousness, and hubris. Others include the relief we feel when we avoid discovery or punishment for acting badly and the pleasure we take in someone else's pain or failure. (The German language actually has a word for this: *Schadenfreude*.)

We work Step Ten with the unshakable knowledge (faith) that we can't live a sustainable life with a primary focus on self. Knowing this, we carefully observe our own emotions on an ongoing basis. We nurture those that, in turn, will nurture a sustainable life and recovery. We also notice those that will not; we take the appropriate actions if needed and then let them go. All the while, we keep in mind that *the more we sustain our recovery, the more it sustains us.*

Overreliance on Self: Two Common Manifestations

In long-term sobriety, some clear differences become visible regarding the expression of the spiritual malady all humans are vulnerable to. Understanding these differences can help us be more self-aware, understanding, and empathetic as we work Step Ten.

The observations I'm about to offer are generalities. They are based on decades of working with many thousands of people in recovery. They're usually true, but not always. There are certainly exceptions, and you might even be one of them.

These distinctions apply across cultures, countries, religions, and races. But they appear in many variations, based on individuals' unique backgrounds. Some of the differences I'll describe in these traits are the result of nature. Some are the result of nurture—how people are raised. Some are the result of cultural forces. Many have a combination of causes.

The two distinct tendencies I've observed in people are that some are more likely to express character defects as selfishness and self-centeredness, while others are more likely to express character defects through self-sacrifice.

In presenting the wisdom of Step Three and what blocks us from having a spiritual experience, the Big Book describes two sets of character traits on page 61. Here is the first:

> This actor may be quite virtuous, kind, considerate, modest, generous, patient, even self-sacrificing.

When we express these positive traits in the right balance— along with others such as assertiveness and self-care—then those traits are very healthy. But when they are over-expressed, they become character defects. Here is the second set of traits described in that same paragraph:

> On the other hand, he may be mean, egotistical, selfish, nasty, and dishonest.

On page 62, the Big Book provides a third list of tendencies:

> Driven by a hundred forms of fear, self-delusion, self-seeking, and self-pity, we step on the toes of our fellows and they retaliate. . . . The alcoholic is

an extreme example of self-will run riot, though he usually doesn't think so.

Whenever I read these passages aloud in Twelve Step seminars and workshops, my observation is that, in general, more women relate to the self-sacrificing traits and more men squirm at the self-centered traits. Clearly, the Big Book lists many, many more examples of the self-seeking variety than the selfless variety. And I find it noteworthy that there was a significant gender imbalance in the "more than one hundred men and women who have recovered from a seemingly hopeless state of mind and body" (Big Book, page xiii). According to some historians, there were ninety-seven men and four women. This helps me understand the source of the lingering male-gender bias throughout the first 164 pages of the Big Book, before the first-person stories begin.

It's a matter of balance. Any healthy human trait, when over-expressed, becomes a detriment. One person's generosity, when pushed too far, becomes exhausting self-sacrifice. Another person's self-care, when pushed to indulgence, becomes self-centeredness. Either way, a healthy trait becomes a character defect.

Regardless of our motives or methods, when we sacrifice too much of ourselves, nobody is likely to say, "Please stop. You're being too virtuous." They're much more likely to tell us, "This is great—keep it up." Or sometimes, "Do it even more." Whereas most folks encourage those who are self-centered in their efforts to change.

An important part of working Step Ten is observing ourselves for any of these imbalances of self-sacrifice. It's easy to delude ourselves—and others—that what we're doing is compassionate, spiritual, kind, and the trait of a balanced person. But it's possible—and, for some of us in recovery, quite easy—to over-express that aspect of ourselves while ignoring other equally important parts of our personalities.

As we work Step Ten, we learn again and again that any imbalance of character traits can create problems. A life run on self-sacrifice is just as blocked as a life run on self-centeredness. Both imbalances are forms of spiritual illness that prevent a spiritual solution. Both are forms of improper use of our free will. And a life out of balance is always unsustainable and unmanageable.

And remember, "But as with most people, we are a combination of these traits" (Big Book, page 61).

<hr />

Les learns the hard way: Too much self-sacrifice

I've been recovering and sober for twenty-seven years now, and I've been a licensed addiction specialist for over a decade.

At a certain point in my sobriety, I felt that I wanted to make a career out of Step Twelve: " . . . we tried to carry this message to alcoholics, and to practice these principles in all our affairs." Partly I wanted to make a positive difference in the world. Partly, too, I wanted to be in an environment that is based in Twelve Step recovery. So I went through an addiction counselor training program and earned an MA in psychology. Soon afterward I got hired by the county for its detox and outpatient program.

I quickly learned that the job is not actually Twelve Step work. It's case management. The people I work with are usually in bad or very bad shape. Usually they're at the lowest point in their lives. Each week I might experience a moment or two of Twelve Step–style fellowship—that feeling of common peril and a common solution—but that's about it. Mostly it's difficult work with tough cases and a big caseload.

Like most county programs, we're understaffed and underfunded.

That's the downside. The upside is that I love the work. I love the challenge; I believe I'm good at it; and I'm constantly learning a lot.

The other plus is that, from the beginning, my superiors have recognized and rewarded my commitment and the quality of my work. I've gotten a lot of praise, several raises, and a service award. In all, it's been very gratifying.

But in some ways, too gratifying—so gratifying that, a couple of years ago, I lost my balance and my emotional sobriety.

Officially, my job is forty hours a week, but I don't think I've ever spent fewer than fifty. Doing this job well requires that kind of time. I understood this from the beginning, and for years my wife and I have planned our lives around a fifty-hour-a-week commitment.

We were able to keep things in balance until about two and a half years ago. Then two things happened at once. For reasons I still don't understand, many of my cases became especially difficult and time-consuming. Maybe it was just the luck of the draw. Maybe it was because I had a good reputation, so I was given the toughest cases. Regardless, suddenly fifty hours a week wouldn't cut it—not if I wanted to continue to meet my own standards. I figured that things would slow down again eventually, so I bit the bullet and spent more and more of my time and energy at work. Of course, the more hours I worked, the more praise I got from my boss.

But not from my wife. She was upset with me. We'd agreed to host an exchange student from Austria for a year, and she arrived at just about the time things got crazy at work. Just when I was supposed to be spending more time at home, I was doing exactly the opposite.

Looking back, I can see that my life was getting more and more unbalanced—and that I had become addicted to my job. I kept thinking, *Things will settle down any day now.* Only they didn't. They remained challenging and time-consuming—for three months, then five, then eight.

During the fifth month, I stopped going to AA meetings regularly. The time pressure at work was enormous and relentless, and I told myself, *I'm in the midst of this stuff all day. It's almost redundant to go to meetings.* I started substituting my career work for my personal recovery work.

Any addiction professional or longtime Twelve Stepper would immediately see the folly in this attitude. And I *would* have seen the folly in it, had it been anyone else. But I was blinded by my own self-sacrifice and the sense of accomplishment it gave me.

So here I was, juggling too many things and not working on my own recovery.

Then one day I met for the first time with a new client. His name was Bernie F. and he was an Orthodox Jew. He had a long beard and wore a skullcap, a white shirt, and black trousers and jacket. He was a pleasant guy, at least when he was sober and in my office, but he'd wrestled with alcoholism for decades. This was his third time going through detox.

So he and I were talking about scheduling, and I gave him some dates for treatment and aftercare appointments. He started shaking his head. He said, "That won't work. I need to be in synagogue for the High Holy Days."

I just looked at him and said, way too loudly, "You need to be in *rehab*." And then—I don't know what made me say this, because it was so totally inappropriate—"God will understand."

Even as the words came out of my mouth, I knew what a big mistake I was making. But it was too late. In that moment, I suddenly realized how out of balance my life had become. I actually remember thinking, *Look who's turned into Mr. Lack of Resiliency and Tolerance.*

I also knew it was time to do a Step Ten, right then and there. So I said to Bernie, "Wow. Was that ever not the right thing to say. I'm so sorry. Give me a moment, please."

I put my hands on my desk, closed my eyes, and took a few deep breaths. Then I opened my eyes and said, "What I said to you a moment ago was probably painful and insulting. I shouldn't have said it. It's beneath the standards of respect and professionalism that the county sets—and the ones I set for myself. My own life has been difficult recently, and I obviously blew a gasket. But my own difficulties are no reason to treat you disrespectfully."

Bernie actually gave me a small smile. He nodded and said, "Apology accepted. So now, maybe, you can find me some different dates?"

The rest of the meeting went fine. We found dates that would work for him and that fit county guidelines.

But as soon as Bernie left my office, I said a silent prayer. *God, please don't let me do something like this again. Please restore balance to my life. Please remove the character defect of self-will that masquerades as self-sacrifice.*

Projects and Project Managers

If you're in a committed relationship, you may notice another distinction as you work Step Ten.

In long-term partnerships, usually one partner's needs primarily get taken care of. I call this person the project. The other partner, who primarily takes care of the project's needs, can be called the *project manager*.

Projects like being taken care of. Project managers like taking care of them.

This arrangement can be perfectly healthy, since we all go about life getting our needs met through some dominance and some dependence. In fact, it often creates a good footprint for a family. In a generally healthy couple, it generates a balanced partnership out of two people's natural differences.

In a less healthy couple, however, the person with the overdeveloped sense of dependence becomes the 24/7 project, while the partner with the overdeveloped sense of dominance becomes the 24/7 project manager. The classic example is the addict and the codependent.

In practice, things are often more nuanced. For instance, one member of a couple might be the financial project manager in the relationship, while the other is the emotional project manager. One partner might manage most of the couple's relationships with neighbors, while the other manages most relationships with extended family. The roles of project and project manager can also shift over time, for example, in an emergency when one partner has a long-term illness, or as couples age.

In couples—especially those with kids—the project manager is the primary caregiver. In part this is because most primary caregivers are hardwired to protect their kids and their families. And, in most couples, the primary caregiver also serves as the family's project manager in another way, providing much of the emotional security.

In American culture, the role of primary caregiver is often represented stereotypically by a female. Listen to a dozen random country western songs sung by males. Many of them will involve a man struggling to feel emotionally safe and secure through his dependence on a woman.

As we work Step Ten and recovery becomes more and more of a way of life for us, these differences become increasingly visible. Project/project manager relationships—whether balanced or imbalanced—aren't just a heterosexual relationship phenomenon, of course. These roles tend to evolve in all committed couples, whether they're straight, gay, or otherwise. All of us are variations on the same theme: human being.

Latisha: I was Kari's "project"

I'm twenty-seven now, and I started working the Steps when I was twenty-five. I go to Narcotics Anonymous groups twice a week. I had a problem with coke that started when I was in college. I've been clean for over a year and a half, and I have no interest in going back to using or my old life.

I met Kari soon after I stopped using. We've been living together for nine months. We're planning to get married next year, and we'd like to adopt at least one child. Until recently, I'd have to say that my life was the best it's ever been.

Over the past few months, though, things have changed between Kari and me. She's always been 100 percent supportive of my recovery. But recently, she's been more like 140 percent supportive, if that makes any sense.

It used to be, when I had a Twelve Step meeting in the evening, she'd kiss me goodbye and say, "Drive safely," and I'd go to my meeting, and we'd have dinner together afterward. That was great. Now it's still all of that—but if my meeting is at seven, she'll say at six thirty, "You need to leave for your group in ten minutes." And I'm like, "Yeah, I know. It's the same Thursday night meeting I've been going to for the last year."

It would be one thing if I procrastinated, or missed meetings, or made excuses not to go, or was chronically late. But none of those things is true about me. I'm not saying I'm perfect. I have my share of character defects. But routinely being late isn't one of them. Neither is missing meetings.

Things kind of came to a head three weeks ago. I was getting ready to leave for my meeting. As I'm putting on my shoes, Kari shouts to me from the other room, "Hon, remember, there's a detour on Highway 7. You should probably leave for your group now."

So I shout back, "I'm on it." But I'm starting to feel pissed. I mean, I know how to tell time. And she knows that I know about the detour because we'd had to take it just that morning.

I grab my coat and my purse and my keys. As I go to kiss her goodbye, she hands me a notebook and a pen and says, "You can use these to take notes. My brother takes pen and paper to his AA meetings, and he says they're really helpful."

That's when something shifts inside me. I turn to her and say, "Girl, what's up with you? I ain't no eight-year-old."

She looks at me like I called her a whore, and she says, "Don't you want to stay clean?"

At that point I lose my mind. I shout, *"Of course I want to stay clean. But I don't need no 24/7 recovery monitor. So just back off, okay?"*

Now Kari looks like she's been punched in the gut. In a tiny little voice she says, "Tish, have you started using again?"

I throw my purse down. Honestly, I'm feeling ready to *throw* that gut punch. And then a door inside me opens and the words just go torpedo-ing out. *"No, I haven't started using again. And I don't need you to decide for me what I take to meetings or whether I write shit down or not. You can take your goddamn notebook and fold it five ways and stick it."*

Soon we're both crying and holding each other and apologizing, and all the while a voice in my head is going, *What the hell?*

And the really crazy part is, because of it I was late to my meeting.

We both simmered down after that, and we talked again later that night. Kari's thing was basically, "I do so much for you and you don't appreciate it." My thing was basically, "I *don't* appreciate it when it's over the top like that. Stop trying to nag me healthy. I don't want you to be my helicopter mom."

Eventually she told me she was feeling scared because one of her friends, who was in the same AA group as her brother, had relapsed and gone on a serious drinking binge. Hearing that helped me. Then I told her, "Kar, thank you for caring so much for me. But I would appreciate it a lot if you would re-mind me when I'm five minutes late, not before I'm five minutes late." She said okay. Things were kind of shaky for the next week. Then, at the following meet-ing, which was an open meeting, the focus was on Step Ten. A guy told the story of him and his wife, and it was *exactly* like Kari and me. She was loving and sup-portive at first—and then, after a while, too supportive.

And he had an explosion a lot like mine. Then he said that over time he developed some patience and tolerance around what he felt was her nagging. Instead of getting upset, he'd just say, "Honey, thanks for your support." And when he started to get pissed off, instead of yelling at her, he'd just say softly, "Baby, are you really sure this is necessary?" And, eventually, most of the time she'd go, "Um, maybe not."

So I decided to try it myself. A few days ago, Kari started doing her recovery monitor thing, and I smiled and said, "Kar, are you sure that I needed that reminder?"

I swear, she just stopped dead in her tracks and looked like she'd seen a ghost. For a couple of seconds she just stood there, silent. Then she said to me, "Tish, do you think I should start going to CoDA meetings?" That's Co-dependents Anonymous.

So Kari had a wake-up call. I also think she finally understands that I'm almost never late for things.

Working Step Ten

∞◇∞

In our initial practice of the first nine Steps, we lay the foundation for a spiritual awakening that results in the Promises given us in the Big Book (pages 83–84).

> We are going to know a new freedom and a new happiness. We will not regret the past nor wish to shut the door on it. We will comprehend the word serenity and we will know peace. No matter how far down the scale we have gone, we will see how our experience can benefit others. That feeling of uselessness and self-pity will disappear. We will lose interest in selfish things and gain interest in our fellows. Self-seeking will slip away. Our whole attitude and outlook upon life will change. Fear of people and of economic insecurity will leave us. We will intuitively know how to handle situations which used to baffle us. We will suddenly realize that God is doing for us what we could not do for ourselves.

Now, in working Step Ten, we begin the final stage of experiencing a spiritual transformation on an ongoing basis, culminating in Step Twelve. As the Big Book tells us, "We have entered the world of the Spirit. Our next function is to grow in our understanding and effectiveness" (page 84). Step Ten, along with Eleven and Twelve, helps us to stay in the world of the Spirit.

The word *stay* is vitally important. The first nine Steps have now become our way of living. As the Big Book explains, "This is not an overnight matter. It should continue for our lifetime" (page 84).

In earlier Steps, we discovered that the only sustainable solution for us was a complete spiritual change. That change has now been brought about, with the help and guidance of our Higher Power. Step Ten enables us to maintain this change—and readies us for further changes. Many of these will occur privately, in our heart, in a manner not immediately visible to the outside world.

In early Step Ten work, we often say, "Wait a minute. What I just said or did was wrong. I'm sorry. Let me make it right." As we mature in our Step Ten work, however, we need to do this less and less often. We learn to observe ourselves, realize what we're doing, and stop—before we've done much or any harm. With practice and experience, we catch ourselves earlier and earlier—first, after we act; then as soon as we act; later, as we begin to act; and eventually, before we act, at the moment of impulse or emotion.

When we did our initial moral inventory, we saw our shortcomings and character defects as painful objects that needed to be removed, like cancerous tumors. Now, however, our vision is clearer, our insight deeper, and our discernment stronger. We see that our character defects and shortcomings are processes, not objects. They cannot simply be discarded and forgotten. They can arise at any time and in any situation. Old flaws that we thought we had grown out of long ago can unexpectedly reappear; so can flaws we didn't realize we had. Unresolved or previously unexamined resentments, fears, guilt, shame, and remorse can all still show up. And when they do, we need to deal with them promptly, as a necessary part of our ongoing recovery.

In working Step Ten, we accept these as natural parts of being human. We do our best to notice them when they arise, and address them as quickly as possible by working Steps Six and Seven.

We have also learned that our character defects and shortcomings are not inherently wrong or bad; they are simply over- or under-expressions of our human nature. We do not ask our Higher Power to remove our desire to be social, or sexual, or safe. Instead, we ask our Higher Power to remove our desire to express those desires in harmful and unsustainable ways.

Amahl: I was tempted to stray—and then I beat myself up for it

I used to be a serious pot smoker. I lit up pretty much every day, sometimes two or three times. I was also a pretty heavy drinker. Am I an addict? At a certain point I decided it didn't matter—I just needed my life to be manageable. I needed to do something before everything fell completely to pieces. That's when I started going to MA (Marijuana Anonymous) and AA meetings.

The Program has worked well for me. I've been drug- and alcohol-free for just over three years. Life isn't perfect, but it's good. And it really helps to have a clear head.

Here's what happened just two weeks ago. I'm reading in the library, in one of its big cushioned chairs. I feel something shift in my pocket and fall out. So I stand up and, sure enough, my keys are gone.

I pull off the bottom cushion of the chair. There are my keys—along with a bag of weed, maybe half an ounce.

My first thought is, *Wow, it's a gift from the gods.* My second is, *Don't be an idiot. You know you'll regret it if you light up.* My third is, *I don't have to smoke it. I can sell it. If it's good stuff, it's worth sixty or seventy bucks.* All this goes through my head in about two seconds.

Then my good sense returns. I stuff the bag and my keys into my coat pocket and head for the men's room. I dump the pot into the toilet and flush it.

I go back and start reading again, but now I'm feeling *really* uncomfortable. How could I even *think* about using again? Or worse, dealing? I feel like I've committed some terrible Twelve Step sin. And then I think, *Have I just taken the first step toward relapse?*

I take out my phone and call my sponsor. I say to him, "Brent, can you talk? I feel terrible, like I just stole toys from Santa Claus or something."

He laughs and says, "Okay, tell me what happened."

So I tell him the story and say, "I know I need to do a Tenth Step about this. Can you help me think it through?"

Brent is silent for a couple of seconds. Then he says, "Working Step Ten is a good idea. But I'd say you've only committed one wrong, and it's not the one you think. You're trying to punish yourself for being human."

This is completely not what I'm expecting. I say, "Come again?" My sponsor says, "Remember what the Big Book says? *If tempted, we recoil from it as from a hot flame.* That's exactly what you did. Nothing in the Program says that it's wrong to feel tempted. In fact, the sentence I just quoted implies that we likely *will* be tempted. That's what I love about the Program. It allows us to be human. It *assumes* we're going to be human. It doesn't demand perfection. It focuses on spiritual progress, not spiritual perfection."

I say to him, "So it's not a shortcoming to be tempted?"

"No," he says. "It's a shortcoming to *act on* that temptation. But, you know, it's also a shortcoming to expect that you'll never be tempted. You're showing yourself too little compassion and understanding. That's something worth asking your Higher Power to remove."

In my head and heart, I did a Step Ten right there in the library. I also found a copy of the Big Book on the shelves and looked at what it had to say about that Step. On page 85 was a sentence I'd read many times before, but had never really thought much about. *We are neither cocky nor are we afraid.*

I had gotten afraid—afraid that I was losing my sobriety because I'd felt a moment of temptation.

Promises, Directions, and Warnings

The Big Book provides us with specific directions for working Step Ten, as well as some clear promises and warnings. When we follow its directions, we live into the promises. When we don't, we live into the warnings.

On pages 84 and 85, the Big Book promises us eight outcomes, which I've numbered here as a list.

1. And we have ceased fighting anything or anyone—even alcohol (or any other addiction).

2. For by this time sanity will have returned.

3. We will seldom be interested in liquor [or whatever substance or activity fueled our addiction].

4. If tempted, we recoil from it as from a hot flame.

5. We react sanely and normally, and we will find that this has happened automatically. We will see that our new attitude toward liquor [or any other addictive substance

or activity] has been given us without any thought or effort on our part. It just comes! That is the miracle of it.

6. We're not fighting it, neither are we avoiding temptation. We feel as though we had been placed in a position of neutrality—safe and protected. We have not even sworn off.

7. Instead, the problem has been removed. It does not exist for us.

8. We are neither cocky nor are we afraid.

The Big Book goes on to tell us that all this becomes the reality of our life, " . . . so long as we keep in fit spiritual condition."

How do we stay in fit spiritual condition? By living according to these clear directions (page 85): "Every day is a day when we must carry the vision of God's will into all of our activities." Instead of constantly asking *What do I want?* as we did when we lived in the grip of self-centeredness, we ask,

"How can I best serve Thee—Thy will (not mine) be done." These are the thoughts that must go with us constantly. We can exercise our willpower along this line all we wish. It is the proper use of the will.

The Big Book has just warned us that because we now live in the world of the Spirit,

. . . It is easy to let up on the spiritual program of action and rest on our laurels. We're headed for trouble if we do, for alcohol is a subtle foe. We are not cured of alcoholism. What we really have is a daily reprieve, contingent on the maintenance of our spiritual condition.

And that's true not only for alcoholism, but for any addiction, including our addiction to self-centeredness. Self-reliance, self-sacrifice, and other forms of self-centeredness are also subtle foes. Because they can creep in in exactly the same way, we need a daily reprieve from these as well. Step Ten is the ongoing practice that, day by day and moment by moment, prepares us for that reprieve. As the Big Book reminds us on page 83, "The spiritual life is not a theory. *We have to live it.*"

Corey: I was complacent—and then I worked Step Ten on my knees

If you live in Portland and you're in recovery, you might have met me, or at least heard of me. For a few years, I was a popular speaker at AA gatherings.

I'm in my fifties now. The time I want to tell you about was when I was in my late forties. I had eight years of sobriety, and almost nine of working the Program. I'd been a sponsor for half a dozen folks. Unquestionably, the Program saved my life, my marriage, and my career.

Although I wouldn't have put it this way, back then I also thought that it had cured my alcoholism. Any desire to drink had long ago disappeared. I would go to parties, or jazz clubs, or restaurants where everyone was drinking alcohol, and I had no problems. Occasionally I'd marvel at how immune most people seemed to be to the disease of alcoholism, but otherwise I'd feel fine, and serenely drink coffee or tea.

At the time, I was at the peak of my career, although of course I didn't know it then. I'm in industrial sales, and I was doing very well, making a six-figure income. And I was happy. The pain of addiction was gone. I'd made all the amends I could. Things were back on track with my wife and my kids. They'd all seen my life turn around, and they all told me they were proud of what I'd become. I was volunteering as the assistant coach of our church's junior high softball team, and that was fun and rewarding too.

Then one morning I threw my back out. I could still walk, but just barely. I went to an osteopath, and she said, "Corey, you're not a kid any more. If you want to keep this from happening again, you need to be exercising regularly. You need to do some cardio and some weights." Which was fine. I'd walk and I'd work out. But walking and working out take time.

I'm embarrassed to admit this, but I remember thinking at the time, *Okay, then. I'll swap some of my AA activities for exercise. I'll just be shifting from one form of self-care to another.* I even remember thinking, *My alcoholism isn't a problem anymore, but my back is. I need to make this switch.*

That's the brilliance of the disease of alcoholism. It distorts your thinking so badly that you actually think your rush toward relapse is something you're doing for your health.

First I stopped the AA speaking, and going to AA roundups and conferences. I told myself that some day I'd start those again. But I kept going to two meetings a week.

Things were still okay. My life was work, family, exercise, coaching, and meetings. It was still a very good life.

But something surprising happened. I liked walking, and I *loved* working out. The walking was relaxing and meditative, and working out pumped up my endorphins. I always left the gym feeling fantastic.

Plus, I was getting stronger every day. I lost eight or nine pounds too, and that also helped my back.

I'd started by walking every other day and working out twice a week. Soon I was walking daily and going to the gym three times a week, sometimes four. I wasn't exactly buff, but Charlene told me I looked sexier and more handsome.

I'm sure you know where this story is headed. After a few months, I cut back to one meeting a week, then to one whenever I felt I could squeeze it into my busy schedule.

And the fact was that I was feeling better than ever. I still had no desire to drink. But somewhere inside me I hadn't forgotten that alcoholism has no cure. And neither does self-centeredness.

After I'd been working out about four or five months—and more or less stopped going to meetings—people began to mention things to me. One night my wife asked me if I was feeling okay. I said, "Sure. Why?" She said, "You don't seem as upbeat or as relaxed as you used to."

It was the same at work. One day my boss asked me, "Hey, Corey, are things okay at home?" I said, "They're great. Why are you asking?" He said, "Well, in the last couple of months you haven't seemed as focused." I just said, "Thanks for the feedback. I'll work on that."

Then, one day after softball practice, Anthony—the coach—called me over and said, "Corey, what the hell is up with you today? You've had your head up your ass all afternoon."

My jaw dropped. I thought I'd been doing fine, doing all the things I was supposed to. I just said, "What do you mean?"

Anthony said, "You kept jumping right down those kids' throats, man. The minister's son was on the verge of tears. You're not training Olympic athletes; they're just here to learn teamwork and have a good time."

That hit me hard. I apologized and thanked him. That same day, as soon as I got home, I got a call from Douglas, one of my sponsees. We hadn't talked in a long time. He said, "Corey, I really miss you. I've kind of been keeping track, and you haven't been at our home group in four months. Are you okay?"

"Yeah," I said. "At least I think so."

We talked for a while, and then he said, "Tell you what, I'll buy you an early dinner on Thursday, and then we can go to our home group meeting at six. I'd be so proud to go back with you." I told him sure, that sounded great. And it did sound great. I figured I'd go straight from softball practice to dinner, and then to the meeting.

On Thursday afternoon, practice went pretty well until about halfway through, when one of the younger kids twisted her leg sliding into home. She lay there in the dirt, bawling her head off. Anthony and I did all the normal first-aid interventions, but none of it helped. She'd probably torn a muscle or even broken a bone. Anthony called her parents and I hustled her off to the emergency room.

We spent a couple of hours in the ER. It turned out to be a partially torn calf muscle. By the time her father arrived and I felt okay about leaving, it was almost six o'clock. I was feeling tired as hell, so I just drove home.

Now I had my cell phone on me the whole time. At any point I could have called Douglas and said, "I'm really sorry. There's been an emergency and I'm with a kid in the ER. Let's try again next week." But I didn't. I didn't call him at all.

I could also have gone to the restaurant. I'd have been late, but I could have explained the situation, and we'd have had dinner and gone to the meeting.

But I didn't do any of those things. I just didn't show up. I blew off my sponsee. And you know what? A part of me was 100 percent aware of what I was doing.

The next morning, Douglas called me. He said, "Hey man, I missed the meeting because I was waiting for you at the restaurant for you. What the hell is wrong with you?"

Suddenly I was infuriated. I said to him, "You know what? You'd better add Al-Anon to your Twelve Step meetings, because you sound awfully miserable based on what another alcoholic is doing or not doing." And then I hung up on him.

That night I went to a bar and drank seven beers. At least I had the presence of mind to walk home instead of drive.

When I woke up the next morning, my wife and kids were gone. Charlene had left a note for me that said, *Call me when you've stopped drinking. I hope that's soon. The kids and I will be at my parents' house.*

I couldn't believe I'd gotten so sick so fast.

But, of course, it wasn't so fast at all. My chemical relapse was only half a day old, but my spiritual relapse had been going on for months.

I took a shower, all the while saying aloud, over and over, "Step One. Step One. I'm back on Step One."

As soon as I was dressed, I went online and found an AA group that would meet later that morning.

Then I made a point of getting down on my knees and putting my forehead on the floor. I asked God to remove my selfishness, my foolishness, my thoughtlessness, and my complacency.

Then I made several lists—of how I'd harmed my wife and kids, my sponsee, the kids on the softball team, and my boss and coworkers.

And then I picked up the phone and started making phone calls. The first two were to Charlene and Douglas. To each of them I said, "I'm so sorry. I've been a total jerk. Can you talk?".

Step Ten and Now

When we did our first moral inventory in Step Four, we looked at how we had harmed others—days, weeks, months, years, and perhaps even decades ago. Then, in Step Nine, we made amends to as many of those people as we could. We cleaned up a great many old messes.

Now, as we work Step Ten, we don't have to spend so much time cleaning up past messes. As a result, we are able to focus on the present instead of the past.

Focusing on the present means being fully engaged, here and now. We're not regretting or reliving the past, or anticipating or worrying about the future. We're fully *here*. This allows us to more clearly see and feel and realize what's going on. We become able to spontaneously work Steps Four through Nine on the fly. Step Ten *is* Steps Four through Nine, wrapped into a continuous activity.

In working Step Ten, we steadily build the habit of doing Steps Four through Nine whenever circumstances require it of us. We no longer work the Steps as a careful, highly deliberate performance. We practice them as on ongoing improvisation on the theme of *Thy will be done*. Eventually, Step Ten becomes a practice, one day at a time, one breath at a time, and one moment at a time.

Observing Our Emotional Selves

Our emotions offer us a continuous opportunity to know if what we're doing, thinking, or planning is sustainable or unsustainable. They give us immediate and constant feedback about how we're using our free will—or how we're about to use it.

Our emotions are also very reliable indicators of when we need to practice Step Ten. Whenever an unsustainable emotion arises, and stays with us more than briefly, that's a sign that Step Ten is called for.

As we practice paying attention to our emotions day by day, we get a very accurate measure of what's working in our life—and what's not.

In Step Ten, as *we continue to watch for selfishness, dishonesty, resentment, and fear,* we learn to become better observers of ourselves. With practice, we get better and better at these directions:

1. Noticing any harm we create *as soon as we create it*— and making amends as soon as possible.

2. Recognizing unsustainable thoughts, emotions, and impulses when they first appear.

3. Noticing ever smaller and more subtle manifestations of those emotions, thoughts, and impulses.

4. Intuiting the probable outcome of embracing or following each one.

5. Restraining ourselves from doing harm to ourselves and others.

6. Asking our Higher Power to remove whatever short-comings and character defects we observe—and to give us guidance for what to do next.

7. Acting out of the best parts of ourselves—with the guidance of our spiritual direction—instead of from our self-direction.

In working Step Ten, we apply our free will by choosing hich thoughts, impulses, and emotions to act on and which ones to let go. We quickly let go of unpleasant and unsustainable emotions as if they were a hot flame. We also recognize that certain pleasurable emotions—self-congratulation, excessive pride, superiority, and their counterparts—as just as unsustainable as jealousy, rage, resentment, or self-pity.

As a result, as we work Step Ten, our transgressions become less frequent. When we do fall prey to the subtle foe of self-interest, we generally create smaller crises and less damaging situations—and we usually learn something important from them. We still make blunders—perhaps even a major one—now and then, but we know how to handle it when we do.

Clarissa: Letting go of a very old resentment

People tell me I have every reason to be angry at my dad, because he molested me regularly for six years—from when I was seven until I was twelve.

I tell them, "No. I have every *right* to be angry. But I have a very good reason not to stay in anger and resentment." Then I tell them the story I'm about to tell you.

I'm not going to give you the details of how he molested me. I'll just say it's not pretty. It happened dozens of times—whenever my mother was out of town. The details are mostly what you'd imagine—except that usually Dad was drunk or stoned.

The other pertinent detail is that my mom died of lung cancer when I was nineteen. She smoked two packs a day from the time she was a teenager, and she never slowed down until the last few months of her life.

The story I want to tell took place last summer, when I was forty-two. I hadn't seen or spoken to my father for almost twenty years, when I ran into him unexpectedly.

I live in a small town in Missouri about fifty miles from where I grew up. I teach high school English. I like my job and I love having summers off.

I also love being clean and sober. From high school until five years ago, I put all kinds of shit into my body—meth, coke, crack, quaaludes, and lots and lots of alcohol—but never heroin, thank God. I'll receive my five-year sobriety medallion next month.

Being clean and sober has meant not having to live in hell. I'm very grateful for that. But until about two years ago, I wasn't very happy either. I've done plenty of therapy, and all kinds of healing strategies—EMDR, somatic therapy, massage, reiki, tai chi, yoga. They all helped me to come back to my body. But they didn't help me with my anger and resentment. Those emotions kept living inside me like rats inside the walls of a house.

Early one morning last summer, I was rereading the story "Freedom from Bondage" in the Big Book. That really struck a nerve in me. In that story, a woman feels like she's being eaten away by resentment toward her mother. I'd read it before—a couple of times—but this time a voice in my head said, *That's me.*

I closed the book. That same voice said, *Enough. I've had enough. Dad already screwed up my life big time. I don't want resentment and anger to screw it up more.*

I started crying—and I couldn't stop. I must have cried for ten minutes straight.

And you know what? After all those tears, afterward I was just as angry and resentful as before. That's when I knew I couldn't heal on my own. Even if I tried every type of therapy in the whole goddamn world.

I opened the Big Book again, to the Steps on page 59. I bowed my head and said aloud, "God, I have to have your help. Please take away my resentment and anger at Dad. I've kept him out of my life, but I can't keep him out of my head." And then I said something I hadn't even consciously realized: "I don't know if I can keep feeling this way without drinking or drugging again. Thy will be done."

I felt a little better after that, so I wiped my eyes and drove to a restaurant downtown that makes really good pancakes.

I was sitting in a booth by the window, drinking coffee and waiting for my food, when a beat-up station wagon pulled up outside. The driver's door opened and an old, obese man got out—very slowly. It looked like he had serious arthritis, or some other problem with moving. He kept trying to pull himself up out of the seat, without success.

I thought, *There's someone who needs some help,* so I slid out of the booth and started to go outside to help him.

And then, after a few steps, I realized—*it was my father.* Much older and much heavier, but definitely him. And what I felt for him right then was sadness. Just sadness. And a little twinge of pity.

At that point, he managed to stand up, close the car door, and take a couple of steps. He didn't look in my direction, and for a second I thought he was going to come into the restaurant. But he walked past the door and down the sidewalk. And then I lost sight of him.

I sat back down in the booth and said silently, *Thank you, Father.*

I have some compassion for my father now. At times I still have flashes of anger or resentment toward him—but when I do, I immediately say a prayer: *God, please take this away.* And soon the feelings blow away.

I'm not interested in forgiving my father or reconciling with him. But I *am* interested in having a life—and I'm doing my best to have one, with the help of my Higher Power.

Suppose that you wake up on a Sunday morning and review your plan for the day. As part of working this part of Step Eleven, you also review your emotions around each part of the plan. *Okay, we're going to have breakfast and read the paper. Nice. We'll also do some chores around the house. It'll be good to get those done. Then I have to write that report for our Monday morning meeting at work. Crap. I don't want to. Not on a Sunday.*

Because you're observing your own emotions, you can see immediately that you're feeling positive, sustainable emotions about everything except the report. You're feeling some resentment about that. But because you immediately recognize that resentment, you don't have to go through the day feeling resentful. You have other choices. You can remind yourself that the resentment is a form of self-interest, and let go of it—or ask God to take it from you. You can write the report right after breakfast. By getting it out of the way, you can spare yourself (and your partner) your resentment all day.

When an emotion, thought, or impulse arises, you can also ask yourself this question: *Is following this likely to bring me peace of mind?* With some self-examination, the answer will usually be quite clear. We're never baffled for too long in distinguishing self-will from the will of our Higher Power. When we're attracted to an unbalanced or unsustainable activity, we'll sense that it's not right. We'll recoil in guilt or distaste or unease. That is all the information we need.

We ignore this information at our peril. *One of the greatest missteps in long-term sobriety is having clear insight into what's right and what's not—and then ignoring that insight.*

Our self-observation throughout the day leads us, naturally and seamlessly, into Step Eleven: "Sought through prayer and meditation to improve our conscious contact with God *as we understood Him,* praying only for knowledge of His will for us and the power to carry that out." The book *Twelve Steps and Twelve Traditions* describes this transition beautifully—and makes a solemn promise to us—on page 98:

> There is a direct linkage among self-examination [Step Ten], meditation, and prayer [Step Eleven]. Taken separately, these practices can bring much relief and benefit. But when they are logically related and interwoven, the result is an unshakable foundation for life.

Working Step Ten at Home

Many of us in the Program discover, to our surprise and dismay, that we have the most difficulty working Step Ten with the people we're closest to: the very people we love the most. We are usually much better Step Ten practitioners out in the world, at work and with strangers, than with are with our own families.

This is certainly true for me—even today, after more than four decades of recovery.

There's a good reason for this. The closer we are to someone, the more vulnerable we are to them, and the more easily they can hurt us. Usually there is also some unfinished emotional business: competition, resentment, guilt, jealousy, and so on. As a result, we tend to be more reactive—and sometimes even volatile— toward that person than we would be toward others.

It's not that our closest relationships bring out the worst in us. It's that they bring out a lot *more* of us. This includes more fears, more resentment, more anger, and more reactivity—as well as more love, more caring, more generosity, and more sacrifice.

When I lead Twelve Step workshops, I often ask participants, "How many of you know exactly what to say to your partner (or child, or parent) that would absolutely devastate them?" Invariably, hands go up all around the room. That's how vulnerable we are to the people we're close to.

If a stranger overhears you explaining Daylight Saving Time to your five-year-old daughter and then pipes up, "I didn't understand that, and I bet she didn't either," you'll probably just shrug and try again. But if your partner overhears you giving the same explanation, then walks away with an eye roll, you'll probably feel insulted and angry.

This is entirely normal. It's also a clear sign that you need to practice Step Ten right away.

You can note each of your emotions and then say to yourself, *My loved one isn't trying to insult or attack me, so there's no need to fight back. Anyway, this isn't about me. It's about teaching a useful concept to our daughter. I can let go of these emotions and focus on explaining the concept to her again, in a different way.* And you can say to your Higher Power, *Please take this impatience and emotional fragility away from me.*

That's the ideal. In real life, most of us have had the experience of leapfrogging over every possible mindful response. We growled at our partner, "I suppose you can do much better, huh?"

or "Don't you *dare* roll your damn eyes at me," or "Why don't you just come out and say it? You think I'm a friggin' idiot."

Here's part of the magic of Step Ten: if we do say something reactive and caustic, we haven't blown our chance to work the Step. As soon as the words are out of our mouth, we can still catch ourselves and say, "Hold on. That was a crappy thing to say. I shouldn't have said it. I was feeling hurt and angry, and I lashed out at you. I'm sorry." Internally, we can add, *God, please remove this fear of criticism from me.*

And even if the interaction turns into a pissy, pointless, juvenile argument with your partner, you can still work Step Ten at any moment. As soon as you have the presence of mind—whether it's five seconds later, or five days—you can take a moral inventory, admit your wrongs, ask your Higher Power to restore you to sanity by removing your flaws, and make appropriate amends.

Even though so many of us have a hard time practicing Step Ten with the people we're closest to, *most of us still practice it.* We just tend to practice it after we've made fools of ourselves, instead of before.

But over time, with practice and painful experience, we learn to do better. We catch ourselves sooner. We make smaller and less harmful mistakes, and make them less often. Practice makes progress.

Here's the biggest piece of Step Ten magic: The very moments when you're having the hardest time, and feeling the most guilty and embarrassed, are when you're practicing Step Ten especially well. When you're standing in front of your family, shaking your head and saying, "I'm so sorry; what the hell was I thinking? I was 100 percent wrong; what amends do you need me to make?"—*that's* when you're doing some of your best and most healing Step Ten work.

Violette: Working Step Ten with
my parents in mind

I'm a student at a well-known art school, majoring in painting. I turn nineteen in a couple of months.

I come from an overachieving family. My father's a successful lawyer; my mother's a doctor for the state health department. I'm the youngest of three kids. Both my sisters are very smart and athletic; one went to Northwestern, the other to UCLA. Suzanne is doing her medical residency in North Carolina; Yvette is working as a Congressional aide in Washington. Mom and Dad pushed all of us to work hard and succeed.

Growing up, Suzy and Yvette *did* work hard and *did* succeed. I was the black sheep. I worked as hard as they did, but I just didn't have their abilities, at least in the traditional stuff—top grades, varsity sports, all of that. Through ninth grade I did okay, but nothing special—I mostly got Bs, and a handful of Cs.

I grew up in a small town, so I had the same teachers my sisters did. Like my parents, they expected me to be a clone of Yvette and Suzy—which I wasn't. Still, my teachers all made it clear that I was disappointing them—that I could magically *become* my sisters' clone if I only put my mind to it and tried hard enough. As if it was my fault that I didn't have their talents. The really sad part is that for a long time I believed them.

One night, the summer after ninth grade, my friend Bryant and I bought a few cans of spray paint and sprayed some cartoon figures on a railroad bridge just outside of town. When he saw mine, he said, "Vi, yours is really good. Do another one." So I did, and he went, "Wow, those are both amazing. Really amazing." That's how I got started as a graffiti artist.

And not just graffiti. I did these surreal, colorful portraits and landscapes—Salvador Dali meets Peter Max. I painted on bridges, underpasses, parked railroad cars, abandoned buildings. Always late at night, when my parents thought I was asleep. They didn't have a clue what I was up to.

Bryant was a photographer, and he took pictures of all my art. Not that I could show them to anyone but my friends, since what I was doing was illegal.

Later that summer, I met a couple of other graffiti artists from the area, and we started hanging around together. They all told me my art was really good. They all were also serious drinkers. I started drinking with them. By the end of that summer, I was a fullblown alcoholic.

So now it's October of tenth grade. I'm sneaking out at night with my friends two or three nights a week, doing my art, and then getting drunk. I'm not paying much attention in school, but my parents don't realize it yet, because the first set of grades hasn't come out.

Then, one night, my friends and I get busted as we're painting stuff on the base of the town water tower. Which, looking back, wasn't a very smart idea. The cops catch us red-handed with paint cans and a bottle of Johnnie Walker. They were actually pretty easygoing as they took us in—I mean, we're just a few drunk kids. We're not stealing or fighting with knives. They booked us for underage drinking and defacing public property. And then, of course, they called my parents.

Soon Mom and Dad show up, looking like they'd both strangle me on the spot if they could get away with it. My mother cries the whole time. My father keeps asking me, "How could you do this to us?" As if the whole point of my art is to make him unhappy.

So now I've totally proven to both my parents that I'm a worthless drunken criminal.

But then a funny thing happens. The school district, which covers four towns, has a social worker on staff, and she urges me to go to AA meetings. I figure, my life is complete shit, my parents are ready to ship me off to the Home for Hugely Disappointing Children in Siberia, or possibly someplace worse. What do I have to lose?

There's a meeting on Monday nights at the Methodist church. So I go, and at the meeting, of all people, I see the high school art teacher. He's been sober eleven years. And get this—my friend Bryant has shown him photos of my paintings. After my first meeting, he comes over and says, "Violette, I want you to know that you're very talented. If you want some mentoring with your art, I'm happy to help."

This is the first time an adult has *ever* called me very talented. Including my parents.

Wait. It gets better. I also get separate phone calls from both my sisters. Both of them say the same thing: they're pissed at our parents. They're pissed at Mom and Dad for pushing them so hard and so relentlessly, and for insisting that they achieve in the ways Mom and Dad wanted, not in the ways *they* wanted. They're *delighted* that I'm doing art on my own terms at age sixteen. Yvette just says, "From now on, Vi, do it in ways that are legal, okay?" And Suzy tells me, "Get sober and stay sober and things will get better, I promise. Once you graduate and get out of the house, Mom and Dad can go to hell if they can't appreciate you for who you are." I can't believe those words are coming out of Ms. Perfect's lips.

So now everything starts to fall into place. I transfer from one of my classes into art, and the teacher turns out to be incredibly helpful. He even speaks on my behalf at my Juvenile Court hearing, so I'm sentenced to repainting the base of the tower and doing 100 hours of community service. I've stopped drinking and I'm working the Steps and going to my meeting every Monday.

I'm still a B and C student in most of my classes, but I get straight As in every art class I take. Mom and Dad are still not happy, but they forget about exiling me to the Gulag for Disobedient Teenagers.

The rest of high school goes okay. I work the Steps and don't drink, and whenever I get the urge to cover a wall with graffiti art, I cover my bedroom wall with flip-chart paper and paint on that.

In my senior year I apply to art school, and my art teacher gives me a great recommendation. I get a nice merit scholarship that pays half the cost. Near the end of the school year I have my own senior art show, which goes great. There's even a little article about it in our town paper.

Now my parents are popping their buttons with pride. They tell everyone how talented I am and how they always knew I could do great things. Which is 100 percent bullshit. But I figure, one more summer and I'm gone, so I keep my pie hole shut.

One great feature of my art school is that it's got something called the Student Step Program. You live in a separate dorm that's drug and alcohol free; there's an addiction counselor on staff; and there's an AA and an NA meeting in the dorm every week. How cool is that? I signed up as soon as I learned about it.

So I get to art college, and the first thing that happens is, I've got this long list of requirements to fulfill. Basic, formal training in perspective, figure drawing, art history, yada yada. And I have to tell you, I'm bored out of my freaking mind in every class. It's not at *all* like high school, where my art teacher was constantly challenging me to stretch and try new things. Here no one seems to give a rat's ass what I'm capable of. Instead, they're putting me and every other freshman through art boot camp.

I do my best to keep my nose clean, and I manage to make it through the first six weeks with my body and soul and sobriety intact. But I hate every minute of it.

Then, last Sunday, I'm having brunch at a restaurant with some friends, and one of them orders a mimosa. Her boyfriend says, "Me too," and the next thing I know, I say, "Me too."

Everyone at the table turns and looks at me, and suddenly I feel like the biggest piece of shit that has ever existed on earth. I say, "Wait—cancel that," and I get up from the table and get the hell out of there.

My hands are trembling. I call my sponsor, Tonya, but I get her voice mail. So I leave a message saying "Call me," and I go down to the park and sit on a bench, and I just start to cry like a damn baby.

After a few minutes, I wipe my eyes and call my old art teacher from high school. "I don't get it," I tell him. "They're making us march in formation and do rifle drills here. I signed up for art school and ended up in ROTC."

He laughs and says, "Didn't they explain to you why you need to revisit and refine your basic skills?"

I tell him, "No. They just gave me a list of requirements and said, 'Here's what you have to do.'"

He sighs and says, "Oh boy." Then he spends the next twenty minutes explaining to me the importance of classical training in technique and in the history of art, and how it will support and strengthen everything I do. It all makes total sense. But for some reason, no one at art school bothered to sit me down and explain it.

I do a Tenth Step right then, sitting on that bench. The only harm I did to others was worry the people at brunch. That's no big deal. In a few minutes, I can just go back and apologize. But right now I need to talk to my Higher Power.

Please, I say, *take away my impatience and self-will. Help me trust that my teachers might know what's best for me and please, God, help me tell the difference between my education and my parents.*

A minute later my phone rings. It's Tonya, my sponsor. I tell her what's been going on, and she tells me I did exactly the right thing.

Next time you and your partner (or child, or parent, or roommate) are shouting at each other over something trivial, such as leaving your shoes in the living room, and a voice in your head says, *Am I imagining this, or am I acting like a complete idiot?* that's your invitation to work Step Ten.

And as you work that Step, remind yourself just how far you've come. It's true, you're arguing over something silly and unimportant. But you're no longer arguing over where you hid the booze, or the drugs, or the Visa bill.

The World of the Spirit

A common misconception about Step Ten is that we work it at the end of each day. But the Big Book tells us that we use Step Eleven to review the day when we retire, and review our plans for the day when we wake up. Step Ten is to be worked throughout the day as we put Steps Four through Nine into practice as each situation warrants.

Many of us were taught the following regimen in a Twelve Step treatment program:

Shortly before going to sleep, we review our day—our encounters, our actions and interactions, our decisions, and our emotions and impulses. We do a moral inventory of the day—a short-term Step Four—and list our liabilities and assets. Then we quickly work Steps Five through Eight, and make plans to work Step Nine as soon as we can.

These end-of-the-day reviews are enormously helpful. They keep us humble, and they help ground us in the world of the Spirit. They assist us in recognizing and being honest about our character defects and shortcomings. They help us spot things we may have missed during the day. And they help us continue to become wiser, more compassionate, growing human beings.

But a daily review is always about the past or the future. It is not about *now. And now is when Step Ten becomes fully alive.*

Unlike our first experience of working Steps One through Nine, we don't only practice Step Ten at specific times and in particular places. We work Step Ten as a natural and ongoing part of our life. As the Big Book notes on page 84, "we continue to take personal inventory and continue to set right any new mistakes as we go along."

We need to work Step Ten moment by moment. We don't wait for the end of the day to reflect on what we're doing or feeling. We observe our actions, emotions, and impulses right now. As necessary, we work Steps Six and Seven—or Four through

Nine—right now. We surrender now to the will of our Higher Power and to whatever the moment requires of us.

The world of the Spirit is always now.

The Subtle Power of
the Ripple Effect

∞

The Ripple Effect is the effect we have on other human be-ings, based on what we do (or don't do), what we say (or don't say), and how we show up in each moment. Our words and actions naturally ripple out to the people around us—and then to the people around them, and the folks around them. It's an ongoing interactive process.

Remember the two scenarios about the Ripple Effect from this book's introduction? In the first example, we cut in front of another driver on the highway. The ripples from that one small event eventually resulted in that driver having to declare bank-ruptcy. And that bankruptcy created further ripples: misery for her, difficulties for her unpaid creditors, stress between her and her partner, and so on.

In the second scenario, we smiled at the other driver and waved her in front of us. This rippled out in a positive way for years, helping to support her career success—and, as it turned out, ours as well.

The Ripple Effect is as profound as it is subtle.

Noticing the Ripple Effect

Before recovery, we didn't see the Ripple Effect at all. We were largely unaware of how our behavior affected others. Or, if we were aware, we either denied or ignored the impact we had, or we simply didn't care.

Early in our recovery, we may not have recognized the Ripple Effect very well. We were focused primarily on our own healing, sanity, and serenity. These were worthwhile goals, of course— but they were still self-oriented.

By the time we did our first Steps Four through Nine, however, we had begun to see how our life and the lives of others are inextricably interwoven. When we first worked Step Nine, we understood this well enough that we didn't make amends just so we would feel better. We did it because we recognized that our decisions, words, and actions had harmed other people.

Now, as you work Step Ten in your own recovery, you will start to see how *all* your decisions, words, and actions ripple out and affect others. You'll also notice how everyone else's decisions, words, and actions ripple out in the same way.

The Ripple Effect: Part of the Fabric of Life Itself

In his history of AA, *Not-God*, Ernest Kurtz saw the Ripple Effect at work within each AA group. He described it as "the shared honesty of mutual vulnerability openly acknowledged."

Maybe you remember a popular movie from the year 2000 called *Pay It Forward*, starring Kevin Spacey, Helen Hunt, and Haley Joel Osment. It offers a moving look at the Ripple Effect in action—as well as an honest depiction of the disease of alcoholism.

As you continue working the Program, the Ripple Effect will become more and more visible to you. Eventually you will see it functioning everywhere at all times. It will seem at once magical and utterly ordinary. It will seem so clear to you that you wonder how people can miss it.

The Ripple Effect in Action

The most obvious form of the Ripple Effect involves our words and actions.

Suppose you repeatedly lie to your business clients or provide them with mediocre service. Because they've learned not to trust you, you lose their business. Your income shrinks. Soon you're unable to continue paying for your son's tuition at the private college four states away. He has to drop out, leave his girlfriend behind, move back in with you, and go to community college a mile away. A few months later, his girlfriend tells him, "I just can't do a long-distance romance. We're done."

The entire trajectory of your life, and your son's, has changed because of how you treated your clients.

Let's turn that around. Let's say you consistently provide your customers with good value at a fair price. Your business grows. Your son graduates from the private college with honors and marries his girlfriend. Her father becomes an angel investor in your company, which enables it to grow and become even more successful. Once again, the entire trajectory of two lives has changed because of how you treated your clients.

By now you've probably noticed that even small changes in what you say and do can sometimes have profoundly different effects on other people. For example, there's a difference between asking someone with curiosity and concern, "Are you upset with me?" and asking them the very same question with defensiveness and irritation. The first tone of voice is likely to encourage a concerned, caring response that can lead to a resolution of the problem and closer relationship with that person. The second may encourage an angry or dismissive response that escalates into further conflict and alienation. If you've done a Tenth Step before you ask, identifying your feelings of fear and defensiveness before you ask the question, and asking your Higher Power to remove any defects associated with those feelings, then you're more likely to be fully present and genuinely want to know if you've done something to upset that person.

I've created these simplified examples simply to illustrate how the Ripple Effect works. Real life is of course more complicated and nuanced. Most events have multiple causes and an even larger number of effects.

On any given day, most of us make hundreds of small and large decisions, act in hundreds of different ways, and say hundreds of different things to a wide range of people. Each interaction and conversation has its own Ripple Effect, and we can't control them all. What we can do is—after having cleaned house with Steps Four through Nine—*relax*, knowing that we now have the insight and tools with Step Ten to face each day and moment with openness and serenity.

Emilio: Toasting our marriage with Mountain Dew

It's been nearly seventeen years since I last drank alcohol.

I think it's fair to say, though, that I'm a practicing caffeine addict. It's been an on-and-off thing for me. I'll go for a few months drinking a lot of it. Then I'll be abstinent for a few months to a year. Then I'll cycle back into lots of caffeine. Usually it's coffee, sometimes diet soft drinks or tea.

I've had three sponsors over the course of my recovery, and they all said things like, "So you're a caffeine addict—just like lots of us. Big deal. Just drink your coffee and tea black, and stick to diet soda."

It's weird to get approval for an addiction from my fellow Twelve Steppers, but I understand it. The caffeine does no harm and has no calories—and it helps us stay sober.

This spring, soon after my wife Judy and I retired, I started drinking a lot of diet Mountain Dew—usually two or three a day. I just find it really refreshing, particularly on hot days.

At first Judy disapproved of my drinking so much of it. She said the extra caffeine and the aspartame aren't good for me. Which is probably true. But they're way better than alcohol.

She and I drink plenty of coffee together—usually a couple of cups in the morning and one in mid-afternoon. I drink the diet Mountain Dew in addition to the coffee.

For the first few weeks I drank the diet Mountain Dew in front of her. But she'd give me this look—the same look she used to give me when I drank alcohol. She'd look at the can in my hand, and then at my face, and then back at the can. She wouldn't say anything, but I could feel the disapproval just oozing out of her.

So—and I realize how ridiculous this sounds—a couple of months ago I stopped drinking it in front of her. I kept it in the fridge in the garage, and I usually drank it when she was away from the house or in the shower.

At first I felt resentful about her disapproval, but I got over it. I asked my Higher Power to remove it, and it faded away.

But if you have a partner, you know that things are never that simple. She didn't say anything and I didn't say anything, but a distance started to grow between us. Without saying a word, we communicated through our vibes that we didn't fully trust each other.

And there was more going on than just the soda. Judy and I agreed long ago that neither of us would buy anything that cost more than a hundred dollars without the other's approval. But my friend Steve had a baseball autographed by Hank Aaron that he said he was going to sell online. He offered it to me first for two hundred bucks. I knew I could get at least three hundred for it if I ever sold it, so I said sure and wrote him a check. But I hadn't told Judy about it yet.

A few days after that, I bought a case of diet Mountain Dew and hid it behind some tools under my workbench. I didn't feel guilty or anything. I just didn't want Judy hassling me about it. I was afraid she'd blow up at me, and then I'd lose it too—all over some goddamn cans of soda.

Things came to a head the following night. We were having dinner, and just as I took a big swallow of water, Judy said, "Tell me about the two hundred dollar check you wrote to Steve."

I almost spat the water across the room. All kinds of feelings came bubbling up. Anger, guilt, indignation—most of all, fear. Even though I hadn't gone anywhere near alcohol, and had zero desire to take a drink, I felt like somehow I'd been caught boozing.

That's when I stopped myself. I took a deep breath, looked at Judy, and said, "Hon, give me a minute." I closed my eyes, took a few more breaths, and silently asked for spiritual guidance. Then I centered my energy in my heart and reminded myself how much I loved Judy and how important she was to me.

I opened my eyes. She was looking at me over the top of her glasses, like a teacher who'd caught me copying answers off another's student's paper. She raised an eyebrow, waiting for me to speak.

I said to her, as lovingly as I could, "I've been feeling some distance between us these past few weeks. You probably have too."

She raised her other eyebrow and said, "You bet your ass I have."

I let it tumble out. "The check to Steve was for a baseball signed by Hank Aaron that's easily worth three hundred bucks on eBay. I should have discussed it with you first. I'm sorry. If you want me to sell it, I'll sell it."

She put her chin on her hands and said, matter-of-factly, "Uh huh. And what else have you been hiding from me?"

I said, "I drink two or three diet Mountain Dews every day when you're not watching. I just bought a case and hid it in the garage."

"And?" For a split second she looked like she was going to laugh, but she didn't.

"That's all," I said. "Those are my sins." I felt calm—but I wondered if it was the calm before the storm.

Judy cocked her head. She seemed pretty calm herself. "Well," she said, "I suppose that as sins go, those are pretty paltry." Then she stood up, kissed the top of my head, and asked, "You want some coffee?"

At that moment, something shifted inside me. I was totally centered and quiet inside as I stood up. Then I kissed her on the mouth. Then I said, "No. I want a diet Mountain Dew. I don't have the same feelings about it as you do. I enjoy it, and I'm not hiding it from you anymore."

I went out to the garage, grabbed the case, and put it on top of the fridge. I took out a few cans and put them inside.

A week later, when Judy came home from the grocery store, I went out to the garage to help her unload. Sitting on the back seat was a case of diet Mountain Dew.

Life as a Sea of Interacting Ripples

So far, I've discussed the most visible and obvious aspects of the Ripple Effect. But, as you may have begun to discover, there are many other aspects as well. As Step Ten becomes a natural part of your life, more and more examples of the Ripple Effect will become visible. Let's take a close look at some of them.

The Ripple Effect of Your Presence

Behind what you say and do and decide is your presence: how you show up and what you notice in each moment.

Addiction is the opposite of presence. Practicing addicts' behavior disconnects them from other people and removes them from the present moment. Their focus is entirely on themselves— what they want, how to get it, and, if they don't feel good, how to feel better as quickly and expediently as possible. This self-centeredness ripples out into the world in all directions, harming one person after another.

When you first worked Steps One through Nine, all of this changed in your life. Your focus was no longer on serving yourself. It was on accepting the care and guidance of a Higher Power. As a result, you began to show up differently. You started to care about and empathize with other people. You began to live in the present instead of in your grudges and fears from the past or your hopes and fears for the future. All of this rippled out into the world—in a positive way.

Now, as you continue to work Step Ten (and the Steps that follow it), your focus is no longer on your own transformation. It is on serving and carrying out spiritual direction. You are learning to return to the present moment; to pay close, careful attention; to connect with others; to get out of your own way; to ask your Higher Power for guidance; and to follow that guidance.

Or, as the Big Book puts it, "To be helpful is our only aim. . . Helping others is the foundation stone of your recovery" (pages 89 and 97). Day by day, we grow in understanding and effectiveness and service. Eventually all of this becomes natural, even automatic. And all of it ripples out into the in a profoundly positive way—a way that supports others' sanity and serenity.

The Ripple Effect of Your Energy

Remember when you went to your first Twelve Step meetings? You probably met some people you immediately liked, and perhaps envied. They seemed at once serene, humble, down-to-earth, and comfortable with themselves. They had nothing to prove and no axes to grind. Their very presence told you that they had found a way to live effectively in this world. At the time you might have thought, *I want to be like that.*

Some people describe this aspect of the Ripple Effect as the energy or vibrations we generate. Others call it our way of being. In his book *The Sermon on the Mount*, Emmet Fox calls it "the intangible influence that you radiate at large." We're physical creatures, made of matter and energy, so we naturally sometimes pick up on the energy that ripples out from others. You can interpret this as you like. Maybe it's vibrational or energetic, but not scientifically measurable with our current tools; maybe it's purely cognitive, but extremely subtle; maybe it's mystical; maybe it's some combination. Whatever it is, though, it's real—and it has deep spiritual implications for our lives.

Louis: How ripples can affect the workplace

This story involves me and a former boss, who I'll call Evelyn. This took place when she was new to the job and wanted to make some changes. Many of these were good changes. But Evelyn also wanted to change how the duties of my job were configured.

This surprised me, because I'd always gotten good performance reviews from Wally, my previous boss, and good to great evaluations from the people I worked with. It seemed to me that Evelyn was trying to fix something that wasn't broken. Worse, it looked to me like her proposed changes would make me *less* effective—and less happy in my job, because they would give me far less flexibility.

I asked to meet with Evelyn, and I explained to her exactly what I just explained to you. She listened and then said, "I understand. The thing is, Louis, you only get to see the people you work with. You don't get to see the bigger picture. Seeing that is *my* job. I understand that the changes will have some negative effects on you. But they'll support larger positive changes for the organization as a whole. You'll lose some flexibility, but our customers will gain in consistency and reliability."

Despite my decades of recovery, I responded entirely out of self-interest—quickly and mindlessly. I said, "Why do I have to be the sacrificial lamb?" Which was, of course, wildly overstating my potential loss and pain. A better question would have been, *Can we try to find some ways to create that consistency and reliability that will have less of a negative impact on me?*

I don't recall my posture or body language at that moment. But I'm sure my tone of voice was tense, if not outright angry—and I was definitely rippling out unpleasant energy.

Evelyn felt it. She frowned and said, "I don't need you to be Jesus on the cross. I *do* need you to be a team player. That's part of your job description."

This was now officially an argument. I said to her angrily, "I've always been a team player."

She nodded and said, "I know you have. That's one of the reasons you continue to work here. Now please *stay* a team player." She stood up and said, "Louis, this discussion is over."

I walked back to my office. I was seething. Mindlessly, self-centeredly, indulgently seething.

At that moment, I was powerless over my anger and my sense of betrayal. I had also completely lost perspective. Evelyn was asking me to take a real but relatively small hit—to make my schedule more rigid, and to make my life a little more difficult. But at the time I felt like I'd been gut-punched. It didn't occur to me at all to ask for spiritual direction, or to ask my Higher Power to remove my anger and self-righteousness.

Over the next few days, Evelyn and I had two more tense conversations on the subject. As I thought about the changes she wanted to implement, I couldn't see how they benefited anyone—not our customers, not our organization, and not any of the people who worked for it. She seemed to be adding regimentation entirely for its own sake—or maybe just to please herself. At one point I even said as much to her. She responded by shaking her head and saying, "Now I know why Wally resigned."

Then I got a call from *her* boss, LeShaun. Evelyn had gone to him and asked him to intervene. She was as frustrated as I was. To her great credit, she didn't just fire me—although, at the time, I half expected her to.

LeShaun suggested that the three of us meet in his office a few days later. I agreed.

During those few days, I happened to reread one of my favorite passages from Emmet Fox's book *The Sermon on the Mount:*

> If, when someone is behaving badly, instead of thinking of the trouble, you will immediately switch your attention off from the human to the Divine, and concentrate upon God, or upon the Real Spiritual Self of the person in question, you will find—if

you really do this—that his conduct will immediately change. This is the secret of handling difficult people. . . . If people are troublesome, you have only to change your thought about them, and then they will change too . . .

That knocked some sense back into me. I realized what I'd been doing, and I vowed to show up in LeShaun's office giving off very different ripples. I told myself I'd follow Fox's suggestion as closely as I could.

When I got to LeShaun's office, Evelyn was already there. I took a deep breath, mentally asked for spiritual direction, and walked in.

From the beginning, LeShaun treated the two of us as colleagues who weren't getting along, not as boss and subordinate. That helped me—and, presumably, Evelyn—feel safe.

First LeShaun asked Evelyn to explain the situation from her viewpoint. She did, laying out her case clearly and a bit forcefully, but not unfairly. As she spoke, I mentally held her in the purest light of her true spiritual nature. I kept silent and simply sat there—relaxed, attentive, and open.

When she was done, LeShaun asked me to tell my own story. So I did—calmly and straightforwardly, without trying to argue my case or control the outcome, and without getting upset. Throughout it all, I mentally held Evelyn in a kind of spiritual halo.

LeShaun looked thoughtful. He asked each of us one or two follow-up questions. Then he leaned forward and said, "Sitting with me in my office are two caring, committed employees who want the best for this enterprise and for the people it serves. While it sounds like the two of you developed some heat under your collars, it's also clear to me that your disagreement is over how to best be of service. It's not about turf or personalities. I thank you both for that."

Then he offered a solution—a brilliant solution, really—that allowed me to keep 90 percent of my flexibility while also giving Evelyn the continuity and standardization she felt were so important. Plus, it was better for our customers than either the status quo or Evelyn's proposed changes. It was also an idea I would never have come up with on my own.

Then LeShaun said, "Now, if I've heard you both correctly, that should settle your dispute. Does it?" He looked at each of us.

Evelyn and I said "Yes" at the same moment.

LeShaun nodded. "Are there any other outstanding issues that the three of us need to discuss?"

Evelyn and I looked at each other. We both shook our heads.

A minute later, Evelyn and I were walking back to our offices together, chatting pleasantly.

It would have been very easy for me to have brought our little war—and my angry, self-protective ripples—into LeShaun's office. To this day I'm grateful that, instead, I let myself radiate a calm, open presence; told my story simply and straightforwardly; and otherwise kept my damn mouth shut. I'm also grateful that I asked for spiritual guidance instead of trying to wrest control of the situation.

This was an important lesson for me because I can easily get on my high horse about being right.

And here's a postscript: Evelyn turned out to be a pretty good boss—in some ways, better than Wally.

The Ripple Effect Inside You

So far, I've spoken of the Ripple Effect as something that ripples out from one person to another. But as we keep working Step Ten, we learn to notice the Ripple Effect operating *inside* us. This occurs in multiple ways—five, at least.

First, when we're living a life of service and carrying out the will of our Higher Power, we can feel the rightness of it in our own body. (This doesn't mean it always feels easy or comfortable. Sometimes it may feel just the opposite.)

Second, over time we'll not only feel that we are rippling out into the universe, but that the universe is rippling through us, expressing itself through us. This may be accompanied by a sense that we are in exactly in the right place, doing just what we need to do.

Third, as we work Step Ten and our recovery continues, a process of neurological healing takes place in our brain. New neural pathways get created and strengthened; old, harmful ones atrophy and disappear. An internal Ripple Effect literally heals our brain.

Fourth, as we develop our presence and internal awareness, we get better at tracking the subtle processes through which emotions and impulses arise in our body. Instead of mindlessly letting them ripple out through reactivity, we examine them. We discern the needs behind them. We choose our response based on the unique details and relationships of that moment. We work the appropriate Step. As necessary, we ask our Higher Power for help and guidance. We also learn to notice when we are impatient and distracted, not bringing our full presence to the moment. This awareness enables us to do an internal reset— and quickly return to the here and now.

Fifth, we become aware of more and more aspects of our personality that we were blind to before.

The Ripple Feedback Loop

There's an engine that's always on in each of us. This engine creates an ongoing feedback loop of internal ripples that looks like this:

- The condition of my character shapes my thinking.

- The condition of my thinking shapes my decisions.

- The condition of my decisions shapes my actions.

- The condition of my actions shapes my practices and habits.

- The condition of my practices and habits shapes my character.

As we work Step Ten, we steadily strengthen our ability to observe all aspects of this internal process. This helps us make conscious and loving choices, rather than impulsive or fearful ones.

The people who founded Alcoholics Anonymous didn't think in terms of this engine, but they were keenly aware of its elements. Steps One and Two cover our thinking. Step Three covers our decisions. Steps Four through Nine cover our actions. Steps Ten and Eleven cover our practices and habits. And Step Twelve covers our character. Twelve Step Programs offer healing and transformation at every point in this loop.

Other programs for addressing addiction intervene at specific spots in the loop, but not throughout the entire loop. For example, rational behavioral therapy intervenes at the points of thinking and action. Reality therapy intervenes at the point of action. These and other helpful interventions help people stay out of trouble in the short term and change their behavior for the better. But they're not spiritual programs that lead to transformed lives.

The Ripple Effect Inside Others

Because we have developed our own internal discernment, we also get better at noticing the subtle cues others give us about what is going on inside them. We notice their posture and the flow of their gestures. We hear the cadences and tone of their voice. We see the look in their eyes and the way they make (or avoid) eye contact. We cannot read minds, but we can learn to feel the energy of other people's bodies as it ripples out and through our own.

When we observe a change in someone else's presence, we are also able to examine it rather than simply react to it. Why does Jackie suddenly sound protective and defensive? Did I say something that bothered her? But all I said was, "How's your brother doing?" in a friendly tone. Part of me wants to get defensive myself and say something snarky. But that will do neither of us any good. I wonder if something else is going on. The only way I'm going to find out is to check it out. Here goes. "Are you okay? I didn't mean to pry."

This discernment also enables us to recognize when we've acted fairly and compassionately and when we haven't. If Jackie responds to our question with "I really don't want to talk about it," we neither defend ourselves nor blame ourselves. We simply say something such as "I understand," and change the subject.

The Ripple Effect of Events

As we practice Step Ten, we also are open to the ripples of unfolding events—to what psychiatrist Carl Jung called *synchronicity*.

When we were in the throes of our addiction, we tried harder and harder to control events, other people, and ourselves. This proved unsustainable and unmanageable. Eventually we crashed and burned. Now, as our recovery matures, we no longer try to manage and control the world. We know that's impossible. We also know that it can be the road to relapse.

We understand that we simply cannot know what will happen next, no matter what we do. We have seen, many times, events evolve in ways we could never have imagined. We have experienced remarkable, unexpected, and unpredictable turns of events that were perfect for everyone. We have been part of spiritual experiences that we could not possibly have crafted, planned, caused, or controlled on our own.

Eventually we lose any desire to impose our own personal will, because we know that our role in life is to rely on spiritual direction instead of the direction of self (ego) and then to carry those directions out in all our affairs.

What happens to us is important. But as we work Step Ten, we come to see that what's far more important is the integrity of our response to what happens.

What happened to us is our history. The integrity of our response is our future. And, through the Ripple Effect, our response will have an effect on the future of the world.

Iris: A lesson from two golden retrievers

The story I'm about to tell you took place soon after I did Step Nine for the first time. I was just beginning to do Step Ten. I'd been in recovery for maybe five or six months.

I was doing the right things, and feeling good. I had a lot to be grateful for. But on that day—I remember it was a Saturday afternoon—I wasn't feeling grateful at all. My boyfriend Roberto was at his parents' house with our daughter, Ariella, and our black Labrador retrievers, and I was home alone. All of a sudden this terrible funk hit me, completely out of nowhere.

This was a new form of misery for me. It wasn't the misery of a hangover or a craving. Or the misery of guilt because I'd done something thoughtless and mean. It had no source at all that I could see. I remember thinking, *What the hell? I thought I was on a glorious path of joyous and serene sobriety.* I kind of assumed I would never feel bad again. Which, looking back, is silly—but it's how I felt right then.

I also felt like I was exuding misery. I was relieved that Roberto and Ariella weren't home and didn't see what a wreck I was. I finally thought, *Okay, I've got to do something. What can I do?*

I decided to go to the park, just to breathe in some nature and be out in the world.

Almost as soon as I got to the park, a couple of half-grown golden retrievers ran up to me, wagging their tails and licking my hands. I love my Labs, but I love goldens even more. These two were super happy, and they obviously wanted me to throw something. So I threw a stick, and they both went charging after it.

I heard their owner calling them. I looked and saw a man who looked a little like my dad. He was with his daughter, who was about Ariella's age, maybe twelve or thirteen. I could see she had Down syndrome.

I went over to them and told them about my Labs, and the girl got excited. She said, "I adore Labs!" She pointed to the goldens and said, "The orange guys are Bonnie and Clyde. My dad named them after criminals. He's weird." She handed me a stick and picked up one of her own. She said to me, "We need to throw and fetch until they're tired out." I looked at her dad. He just smiled and said, "All true."

The three of us spent the next half hour hurling sticks across the lawn until our arms hurt. By then the dogs had had enough too, and just stood there panting. The girl said to me, "You want to know something? Bonnie and Clyde are both boys, but with their you-know-whats cut off. My dad named them. He's weird."

Her father shrugged and said, "Yup, I'm weird. Okay, Jocelyn, let's blow this pop stand." They leashed the dogs, waved goodbye, and walked off.

By now I was feeling good. The energy of the girl and the dogs was contagious, and all the throwing had released endorphins in my body. I walked home smiling, amazed at what had just happened. My favorite breed of dog had come to fetch me and taken me to a happy family that made me more grateful than ever for my own.

When I got home, Roberto and Ariella were sitting on the porch, singing a Justin Bieber song. I shouted, "Your musical taste sucks!" and threw my arms around them both.

Back to Earth

All of this may sound terribly cosmic or "woo-woo" to someone who hasn't had a spiritual experience. But it's not woo-woo at all. We realize—not just in our head, but in our body—that the Ripple Effect is as normal as breathing or walking or smiling.

Because of this realization, we're naturally more calm, more loving, more serene, more willing to help, and more present than we used to be. Even people who think that the Ripple Effect is esoteric can't help but notice the quality of our presence.

To show you just how down-to-earth the Ripple Effect is, let's look at our needs.

When we practiced our addiction, whenever we felt a need, we demanded that other people meet it for us. We did this through dominance (such as bullying, manipulation, deal-making), dependence (such as people pleasing, flattery, playing the victim), or both.

Now, as Step Ten becomes a natural part of our life, we have grown out of this self-centered orientation. Instead, when a need arises in us, we examine it rather than spring into mindless action. Then we focus on meeting that need ourselves—either through our own actions, by asking for help from someone, or by asking for spiritual direction from our Higher Power.

For instance, imagine that you want to find the right sponsor. You're aware of the need, but you know that you can't magically make that person appear. So instead, you go to lots of different meetings, where you'll have the opportunity to meet many people. At each meeting, you keep an eye out for folks who might make a good sponsor. If someone impresses you in the right way, you introduce yourself to the person and talk for a bit. If this initial interaction feels right, you invite the person to have coffee or tea with you.

But that's not all you do. *You also ask your Higher Power for spiritual guidance.*

We keep in mind Steps Six and Seven and remember that it's not always enough for us to do the right things; often we also have to ask for help, so that the things we can't do on our own can come about.

For example, in your search for a sponsor, you might have coffee at a café with Chris, whom you've seen a few times at meetings. It turns out that Chris is moving to New Zealand in three weeks, so she clearly can't be your sponsor. But after a few minutes, Chris's friend Sabrina comes into the café, spots her, and sits down next to you.

As the three of you chat, you learn that Sabrina is also in a Twelve Step group and has three years of solid sobriety. You go to one of that group's meetings and feel very much at home and like the kind of program that Sabrina is working. A month later you ask Sabrina if she will be your sponsor. She accepts.

None of this would have happened if you hadn't introduced yourself to Chris. That was your doing. But also, none of it would have happened if events entirely beyond your control—and your ability to plan—hadn't taken place.

On the one hand, this sequence of events may seem perfectly ordinary. On the other, it is very much a spiritual experience:

a remarkable and unexpected turn for the better that turns out to be perfect for everybody involved.

We cannot control life. Often we cannot solve our own problems. But we can show up fully, ask the right questions, and open ourselves to unknown possibilities. When we do this, the universe may reveal to us a much better solution than we could have ever designed or imagined on our own.

The Ripple Effect and the Serenity Prayer

The Serenity Prayer is one of the Program's most concentrated sources of inspiration and guidance. It is also one of the most beloved and often quoted. Here is the most common version:

> God grant me the serenity
> To accept the things I cannot change;
> The courage to change the things I can;
> And the wisdom to know the difference.

This version of the prayer sets up a duality: the things we can change and the things we cannot. But the Ripple Effect teaches us that these are not our only options.

In Step One we admitted that our addiction was not something we could cure, or manage, or otherwise change for the better. Then, in Step Two, we admitted that we could not become saner or more spiritual on our own. We also understood that as we worked Steps Three through Nine—especially Steps Six and Seven—we would have a spiritual experience and a transformation would occur. But we also understood that we could not make these things happen. *They would happen to us.*

The Ripple Effect is the opposite of trying to control or manipulate the world. It is about showing up, speaking, and acting in a way that—somehow—sets the stage for positive change, often in ways we can't plan or predict.

In recognition of the Ripple Effect, here's another version of the Serenity Prayer to capture its spirit:

God grant me the serenity
To accept the things I cannot change;
The courage to change the things I can;
And the wisdom to also do the things I can
That will bring about the changes I can't.

This is the essence of Steps Six and Seven. When we work them for the first time, we understand that it is not possible for us, on our own, to get rid of our shortcomings and character defects. Our Higher Power must do that for us.

Yet in order to work those Steps—and for them to work on and through us—we also have to act, by asking our Higher Power to remove those flaws. We have to ask for the necessary events to ripple through us. We make a willful commitment to no longer do things the way we used to—and an equally willful commitment to accept whatever happens next.

This altered Serenity Prayer beautifully embodies this same process and attitude.

The Wisdom of "Every Day"

∞

It took most of us months, or even years, to complete Steps One through Nine for the first time. Beginning with Step Ten, however, our recovery is no longer a series of thresholds we cross and actions we complete. The final three Steps are ongoing and timeless. We are to practice them every day of our lives—which is why the subtitle of this book ends with the words *Every Day.*

This chapter offers an array of practices and activities that can help as you work Step Ten day by day and moment after moment. A handful are my own invention, but I learned most of them from other folks in recovery, and from my participation in Twelve Step groups, workshops, and other gatherings. I'm deeply grateful for all of them.

I think of these activities as *recovery aerobics,* because they strengthen our emotional and spiritual muscles, and because their regular practice tends to bring continued, positive results.

Most of them require no planning or preparation, and are practiced in the moment, as events unfold. Some take only a second or two. You can think of this brief, in-the-moment practices as prayers, or mantras, or simple reminders. There are also a handful of more detailed reflections, which appear at the end of this chapter.

Each activity is a variation on one or more of these themes:

• being fully present, with your internal receptors alert

• stepping back from self-centeredness

• serving other human beings

- asking for spiritual help or guidance
- allowing the universe to reveal to you a much better solution that you could ever have created on your own

Some activities will naturally resonate with you more than others. Use the ones that are helpful to you; adapt or let go of the ones that don't.

Spot Checks

These will help you better handle the things that pop up suddenly during the day—impulses, emotions, conflicts, misunderstandings, and so on.

- *Observe your own actions.* If you realize you've just done something unwise, stop yourself immediately. If necessary, work Step Ten on the spot—apologize; make amends; retrace your steps; begin again.

- *Observe your thoughts.* If you have a potentially harmful thought, catch it before it turns into a decision to act. If a thought is about the future, ask yourself if it's practical and helpful. If a thought is about the past, ask yourself if it's compassionate. As the old-timers say, "If you've got one foot in tomorrow and one foot in yesterday, you're pissing all over today."

- *Observe your impulses.* Recognize that they're not internal mandates that need to be followed. They're just momentary urges that may involve money, sex, food, or safety—or, in some cases, power, praise, status, or acceptance. Evaluate each impulse carefully. Then consciously choose how—and whether—to act on it.

- *Observe your emotions.* Often these will be generated by your thoughts, actions, or impulses. In particular, watch for resentment, fear, anger, and shame. These are the emotions most commonly associated with unsustainable behavior. Remember that you always have a choice: you can act on the emotion in a sustainable way; you can act on it in an unsustainable way; or you can simply feel the emotion without acting on it at all. You can simply let it go, and observe it as it moves through you and blows away like clouds after a storm.

- *Observe any hopes for the future as they arise.* Is the hope associated with sustainable thoughts, feelings, or actions? If so, feel free to make the hope a goal. If not, consider amending it or letting go of it.

- *Watch for* shoulds *and* shouldn'ts. Any time you tell yourself *I should* _____ or *I must not* _____ or *I have to* _____, examine that thought carefully. Most *shoulds* and *shouldn'ts* create shame, disappointment, and failure rather than better results. Try reframing them as likes, preferences, goals, or more positive outcomes. For example, *I shouldn't procrastinate* can become *I'll be happier and more productive if* (or *It would be better if) I didn't put things off.*

- *Notice your discomfort.* Your discomfort is a sign that something significant is happening—or about to happen. Don't reflexively try to end the discomfort ASAP. Instead, investigate its source. Then ask yourself what you can learn from that discomfort. Is there something you need to do differently? If so, do it. Or would it be best to simply accept the discomfort for now, and let yourself feel it fully and relax into it?

- *Notice if you're too comfortable.* Let yourself briefly enjoy the good feelings that come with compliments and accolades. Then let go of those feelings. If you cling to them, they can lead to arrogance or laziness—or otherwise get you into trouble.

- *Notice any spiritual lapses.* These lapses are normal and can take many forms. Essentially, they're periods when you have lost your connection with your design for living, either by what you're doing (such as acting out of self-will) or not doing (such as neglecting practice of Steps Ten through Twelve). If you're honest with yourself, when a lapse occurs—or threatens to occur—you'll quickly notice it and catch yourself. You can then return your focus to the Steps, and to the here and now.

- *Give your full attention to what you're doing.* Are you un-focused or scattered? Are you holding something back for no good reason? Bring all of yourself back to this moment.

Arvette: Nobody's immune from embarrassment

I'm a psychotherapist who has written some well-received self-help books. I give talks, lead workshops, and occasionally appear on radio or TV shows. I'm also an alcoholic with thirty-two years of recovery.

In my AA group, of course, I'm just Arvette C. In some ways I'm not very anonymous, because I mention my addiction and recovery in my writing, and there aren't a lot of Arvettes around. When new people show up to the group, some of them recognize me immediately.

On the other hand, in some ways people *don't* really recognize me. What they see is the respected elder and therapist and author with three decades of sobriety.

What they fail to see is the flawed human being who is wired exactly like they are, and who is every bit as dependent on a Higher Power.

My husband Don and I have been married for over forty years. He was a therapist, too, until he retired a few years ago. Our marriage is a good one, but that doesn't mean we don't have problems. People think therapists lead charmed lives, that we don't struggle with the same crapola they do.

Last March, Don and I were at the annual state AA roundup. I was one of the scheduled speakers. Don and I were having breakfast in the hotel restaurant about an hour before I was scheduled to speak. I noticed the people a couple of tables away—a pair of young men—looking at me. One of them pointed briefly at me and then spoke to his partner. I'm used to people occasionally recognizing me and pointing me out, so I just smiled at the couple and returned to eating and chatting with Don.

Then, a minute later, one of the young men got up and came over. I assumed he wanted to thank me for my books, so I put on a big smile. When he got to the table, he leaned down close to me and whispered, "Ma'am, your dress is tucked into your underwear in back."

My face must have turned the color of a tomato. I reached around and, sure enough, in back, the hem of my dress had gotten tucked into my panties. I stood up partway and fixed things as surreptitiously as I could. I thanked the young man, who said, "No problem," and went back to his table.

At that point I was totally flustered, totally off balance. I looked at Don, who had raised both his eyebrows.

I said to him in an angry whisper, "Why didn't you tell me?"

Don spread his hands. "I didn't notice."

"How could you not notice?" I said.

"How could *you* not notice?" Don asked.

I threw my napkin at him and said, "Screw you."

Don's eyes went wide. I hadn't said anything like that to my husband in decades.

Two words echoed in my head: *Step Ten*. I reached across the table and took his hand in mine. "Oh, my God," I said. "Darling, I'm so sorry. *So* sorry. That was totally wrong of me. I was flustered and upset and embarrassed. I imagined the whole restaurant staring at my butt in my granny panties. What amends do you need me to make?"

Don took a sip of coffee—one of his standard ways to buy time. He frowned and said in a very serious tone of voice, "Two things. Number one, next time you tell me to tuck in my shirt, I'm going to giggle, and you're not going to say a thing. Number two, I want you relax and enjoy your breakfast, and then go and give an inspiring talk."

Let me tell you something. It doesn't matter how long or solid your recovery is, or how completely you've turned your life over to a Higher Power. You're still going to have problems: with your character flaws, especially as they surface with the significant people in your life, and sometimes with your clothing. There's nothing in the Big Book that says all your problems will go away.

Internal Reminders

These are quick, simple phrases you can use whenever you're in doubt, in pain, or in trouble. Recite them silently to help you ground yourself in a spirit of service—and in the here and now.

- *Listen up* or *Pay attention.* Recite this to yourself when you're bored, or when you catch your mind wandering—especially if it's wandered into obsessive self-interest.

- *How can I be most helpful right now?* This is another quick, effective antidote for self-centeredness. Another version is Do the next right thing.

- *Let's get to work.* This is shorthand for *I realize there's something I need to do—an effort or change I need to make. I'm willing to shoulder that responsibility, and I'm not going to procrastinate. I'm starting right now.*

- *Keep it simple.* This classic AA slogan is especially helpful when you're confused or overwhelmed.

- *Don't play God* or simply *Not God.* Use this internal wake-up call when you've put self-centeredness before service—or before the will of your Higher Power.

- *There I go again.* Maybe you just caught yourself doing something unwise. Mentally recite these words, preferably with a forgiving smile, not a shameful accusation. Then stop and work Step Ten. Or maybe you were able to catch yourself just *before* doing something you'd have regretted later. Recite this phrase silently, take a deep breath, give yourself a quick mental thumbs-up, and return to the here and now.

- *Don't go there.* Saying this mentally, or even out loud, will help you nip many potential problems in the bud. Stop where you are and say this phrase aloud to wake yourself up.

- *Pause . . . Relax . . . Take it easy.* Silently repeat this sequence—a variation on the AA slogan *Easy Does It*—whenever you feel tense or anxious. Then follow that prescription.

- *Let go.* Gently say this short version of the AA slogan *Let Go and Let God* to yourself—and then do it. Let go of your fears, your anxious hopes, your wanting to control what happens, and your desire to know or understand everything or get all the answers. Above all, let go of your self-centeredness. Stay open and present, and live into the next unfolding moment, and the next, and the next.

Bob: Healing can take time

It's been eight years since I stopped drinking and nine since my divorce. I've got a son, Dylan, who lives with my ex in Stockton, about 600 miles away. Dylan turned eleven last fall.

I was a binge drinker. My addiction cost me my first career, and it was a big factor in my divorce from Meghan. I wasn't a very good husband. Until I stopped drinking, I wasn't much of a dad either.

But Dylan was and is my son. And until recently, Meghan did everything she could to keep me away from him.

Our divorce was ugly. Meghan told her lawyer, "Bob is a no-good, useless drunk. The hell with him. I want the house; I want everything in it; I want whatever money we have left; and I want sole custody of Dylan forever." The judge said yes to everything, and Meghan took Dylan 600 miles away.

At that point, I had no wife and no son and no job and no house. That's when I hit bottom and knew I had to either jump off a bridge or change my life. That's also when I went to my first Twelve Step meeting.

My first year of recovery was very rocky. But once I was back to work—I started fresh with selling cars, and now I'm the assistant manager of a large dealership—things began to improve steadily. I have plenty of regrets about how I used to be, but I've got a new life, a girlfriend I'm crazy about, and a great home group.

But I still feel a big hole in my life. Dylan.

We talk a couple of times a week, and I see him three or four times a year. It always means flying or driving to Stockton. I've tried to get Meghan to let him come to Boise, but she always says no.

Dylan was so young when we split up. He doesn't really remember his old, drunk, messed-up dad. All he knows is this sober, loving guy who his mother says terrible things about. Part of him doesn't understand why his mother talks such trash about me. Sometimes I have to remind him, "Your mother has every reason to resent the man she was married to. I don't like that guy either."

I did the necessary Step Nine work with Meghan. She was clear about what amends she needed, and I made them all. I'm still making them. I send her a generous amount of child support every month—more than the court requires. She'll talk to me about Dylan when there's something we need to discuss. Otherwise, she keeps her distance.

The thing is, I want more with my son. Meghan knows I'm a very different person from the man she married and divorced. But she absolutely refuses to let Dylan come out here. She says, "Ed, I can appreciate who you've become. But alcoholics sometimes relapse. If that ever happens with you, I don't want Dylan to be there by himself, 600 miles from home." I can't really argue with that. But for a long time I resented it.

The story I want to tell happened a couple of months ago. Dylan called me—which is unusual in itself. We usually talk at times we set up in advance. He was crying. He and Meghan had an old rescue dog, a collie they named Hercules. Hercules was dying, and they were going to have to put him down within the next few days. Dylan was very sad.

We spent over half an hour talking about Hercules, who had been part of their family from the time they moved to Stockton. I asked him to tell me stories about his favorite times with Hercules. I let him talk, and mostly listened, and told him how sorry I was that he was losing a family member.

Dylan asked, "You don't mind that I'm crying, do you?" and I said, "Of course not. People cry whenever those lose someone they love." He nodded and said, "Mom's crying too. She's been great about Hercules, but she's also sad. Mom, are you okay? Dad, I need to go now. Thanks for talking."

After I hung up, I was filled with conflicting emotions. I was pleased to be able to connect with my son, and to be available when he needed me. But I was also a little angry that I couldn't be there to comfort him in person. And I know this isn't fair, but I also kind of resented poor Hercules, who'd been able to spend most of his life with Dylan. And I was angry at Meghan for keeping Dylan and me so far apart. Mostly, though, I felt sad for my son. He was far more important than my anger and resentment. Over the next few days, whenever those feelings bubbled up, I'd refocus my attention on Dylan and his grief.

A week later, Dylan called again. He still sounded sad, but maybe a bit more thoughtful. He said, "We took Hercules to the vet yesterday and had him put to sleep. Not like sleep at night. The vet injected him with something that killed him and put him out of his misery."

I asked him to tell me what had happened, and he told the story in detail. They had set Hercules on an examining table, and he and Meghan had held the dog while the vet gave the fatal injection. Hercules had licked Dylan's hand just before the needle went in.

Dylan and I talked for almost an hour. I asked him if his mother would get another dog for the family, and he said, "I asked her that question too, and she said, 'When we're both ready.'"

Eventually he was talked out, and we got ready to say goodbye. Then he said, "When are you coming to visit? I miss you."

After we hung up, I started crying.

When I was done, I emailed Meghan. I thanked her for taking such good care of our son, and for being so loving and supportive with him during Hercules' illness and death.

An hour later, I got an email back from her. She'd cut and pasted my line about her being loving and supportive with Dylan. Underneath it she wrote, *Back at you. M.*

After that, my resentment toward Meghan was gone.

I called my sponsor and said, "Roy, something really good just happened, but I can't figure out exactly what." I told him the story I just told you, and he said, "It sounds like you worked Step Ten without even realizing it." I said, "Is that bad?" He said, "Hell, no. That's the best way to work the Steps. It means they're in your blood."

External Reminders

Sometimes you need to reach out more than you need to reach in. Here are some phrases to help you quickly connect to the spiritual guidance of your Higher Power:

- *I need your help* or *Please help me* or just *Help!*

- *Please guide me* or *Tell me what to do.*

- *Thy will be done* or *I'll do whatever You say.*

- *Thank you:* a quick and easy way to remember to be grateful for whatever you have, even when there's trouble.

When Someone Is Treating You Badly

No life is free of conflicts. As we work the Program, we try as much as possible to resolve conflicts through listening, loving and mindful discussion, compromise, or a blend of these.

Inevitably, though, conflicts with some people will persist or seem unresolvable. Here are some helpful practices for navigating them:

- *Show the other person the same tolerance, pity, and patience you would cheerfully grant a sick friend.* If you have trouble doing this on your own, ask your Higher Power for help. (You'll recognize this practice from page 67 of the Big Book.)

- *Ask yourself, How can I be most helpful to this person?* If necessary, ask your Higher Power the same question. Once you know the answer, act on it.

- *If a harmful emotion or impulse bubbles up inside you, ask your Higher Power to remove it.* This is the purest, simplest form of using Step Ten to work Step Seven.

- *If you're about to say something you know you'll regret, physically intervene on yourself.* Literally bite your tongue. Or inhale and exhale quickly instead of speaking. Repeat as necessary.

- *Follow Emmet Fox's advice and focus on God.* Imagine the other person as a manifestation of the Divine All. Or picture that person bathed in love and Divine light. Or hold in your heart that person's pure spiritual nature. Or simply beam love in that direction. It may also help to simply ignore what the person is saying.

- *Follow the lead of the recovering addict who wrote "Freedom from Bondage"* in the Big Book (pages 544–553). Think of all the good things you would like for yourself. Then wish—or pray—that the person you're in conflict with would get all of those good things. Do this repeatedly, if necessary.

- *If things keep getting worse, quickly remove yourself from the situation.* Say, "Could you hold that thought? I need to step away briefly and take five." Or "I'm not at my best right now; let me take a minute to collect myself . . . I'll be right back." Then leave. Take a few minutes to mentally review what just occurred and do a quick inventory, say one of the slogans or the Serenity Prayer, or do a quick Step Ten if you need to, and then return. If it's clear that further interactions with the person won't help, go back and say, "I don't think we're getting anywhere; I need to go and maybe we can pick this up another time when we're both in a better place."

- *When all else fails, end the conversation.* Say "I need for us to just end this and move on" or "Let's just agree to disagree." Then walk away. This doesn't solve the conflict, but it usually keeps things from unraveling further.

Jenny: In early sobriety, a moment of truth

I drank and did coke for four years before my partner Andrea said, "That's it. It's either me or the drugs and the booze. You choose." That's when I went into treatment.

I was in an inpatient program in Arizona for almost four months. Our insurance only covered the first sixty days. Andrea wasn't very happy about that.

The program was a good one. At first I tried all of my standard bullshit, and none of it worked on anyone. Which was a relief. It had worked on Andrea up until a few months before she laid down the law.

I went through the usual resistance and denial and withdrawal, and I completely fell apart. My counselors helped me through some dark days. At one point I was ready to kill myself, and they talked me down.

A few weeks into treatment, I started seriously working the Steps.

By the time I went home and shifted into an after-care program, I had worked the first eight Steps, and was well into making amends in Step Nine. I was feeling better than I'd felt in many years. My sanity had returned.

So I get back, expecting a big welcome home, and maybe even a booze-and-drug-free party. But I get nothing of the sort. At the airport, Andrea gives me a peck on the cheek and says almost zip. When we get home, she lets me in, tells me she has errands to run, and takes off again.

At first I figure that maybe she's having a bad day, so I unpack, do some laundry, and make myself comfortable. I tell myself that things will get better.

But they don't. Andrea is distant and suspicious. She obviously doesn't believe I've changed. She thinks I'm either faking it or that the changes won't last, and any day I'll turn into my old asshole drunk and coked-out self again.

When I try to talk about it, she just says angrily, "Not now, okay?" or goes into the other room. As for sex, after four months of celibacy I'm more than ready but Andrea isn't interested.

I mean, I get all this. She's still angry at me for four years of bullshit. She's entitled to her anger. But she's also giving me zero credit for who I've become. It seems to me that she wants me to go back to drugging and drinking.

I talk to Tori, my aftercare counselor, about this. She says, "Jen, you can take the booze and the drugs out of a home, but you can't take the history out of it. Andrea is probably very scared and very confused. You're no longer the person she lived with for years. She adapted to your addiction and your unpredictability. Now that you're sober, clean, sane, and predictable, she has no idea how to act around you. Because you've

changed, she has to, too, if she's going to be in relationship with you. It probably scares the hell out of her."

So I say to Tori, "Here's what I don't understand.
If I'd come back exactly the same person I was before
treatment, Andrea would be angry and resentful because I wasn't any better. But now, *because* I'm better,
she's angry and resentful."

Tori just laughs and says, "Welcome to recovery.
Are you working Step Ten?"

At this point I feel like working Step Ten 24/7.
I'm trying hard to walk the line between responsibility and codependence. Every time I do anything
wrong—forget an item at the grocery store, misplace
my keys, leave the basement light on after I come back
upstairs—I say to Andrea, "My bad, hon. I'll make it
right." Usually she just shrugs and says, in a robot-like
voice, "It doesn't matter."

So now *I'm* starting to get pretty pissed off too.

Finally, after about two weeks of being home,
we're sitting on the couch watching a movie—it was
Moonstruck, with Cher and Nicolas Cage—and I reach
over and take her hand. She quickly pulls it away. And
then something opens up inside me.

I grab the remote, turn off the video, and stand up
in front of her. I start to talk, in a voice I barely recognize—strong and calm and 100 percent serious. I have
no idea what I'm even going to say. The words are just
coming, without my thinking them.

I say, "Baby, for years I treated you like crap.
I've told you that several times, but maybe I haven't
told you enough. For all those years I was a *total self-
centered jerk*. I have no idea why you put up with me for
as long as you did. You deserve much better.

"Now I'm trying as hard as I can to *be* the person you deserve. I'm working the Program day by day, going to meetings, and trying to be a decent human being. I'm going to screw up sometimes, but when I do, I'll hold myself accountable and make amends. Maybe it's already too late. Maybe I've hurt you too much, done too much damage. If that's what's going on, just tell me, and I'll pack up and clear out."

Then I shut up. I just stand there, breathing hard. I've got no more words.

For a couple of seconds, it's like we're both frozen in place. Then Andrea starts to sniffle. Then she leans over and starts to sob. Then she starts to *howl,* like a dying animal.

I'm standing there in shock. Andrea is bent over, tears pouring out of her eyes, making noises I've never heard a human being make before. Meanwhile, I'm thinking, *It sounds like someone's being murdered. The neighbors must have called the police by now.*

Andrea falls on the floor, still howling. She starts shaking so hard that I wonder if she's having a heart attack. That's when the question forms in my head: *How can I be of service right now?*

I get down on the floor beside her, wrap my arms around her from behind, and hold her hard and close for the next five minutes, while she cries and shakes and makes animal noises, until finally the pain has worked its way through her.

And that's what it took for things between us to begin to heal.

At the Beginning and End of Each Day

A variety of Step Ten inventory sheets are available for recovering people to fill out at the end of each day. These ask questions such as *How was I selfish? How was I resentful? How was I dishonest? How did I demand control? Who did I hurt and how? Did I keep any secrets? What could I have done better?* and so on. (For samples, type "Step Ten inventory" into your search engine.)

These inventories can be very helpful, especially for people just beginning to work Step Ten. But this programmed approach can also limit how people view the Step.

Here are some other options for making the most of predesigned inventories:

- Add some personalized questions and create your own process for working with them. For example, if one of your character defects is excessive self-sacrifice, you might add to your inventory *How many times today did I say "I'm sorry?"* If you tend to dominate conversations, add the question *How many times today did I interrupt people?* If you're quick to focus on self-interest, add the question *How many times today did I ask myself, "What's in it for me?"*

- Each morning, review your inventory questions—not as a review of your own past actions, but as a way to help ground and orient you for the day. Then mentally walk through the day to come, reviewing your goals, hopes, and plans. Note any potential trouble spots and reflect on how you plan to handle them.

- Post your inventory in a prominent place in your kitchen, or above your desk, or as your screen saver. Each day, simply review it for thirty to sixty seconds. Let the questions sink deeply into you, day by day, until they become a part of you.

As you continue to grow into the Steps—and as they take deeper root in you—even the words *every day* will take on new meaning. You will move from working Step Ten daily, to working it whenever it can be helpful, to living the Steps at all times. Eventually, living the Twelve Steps will become as natural and automatic as breathing—something you do not just every day, or day by day, but moment by moment, in every moment.

Your life will then no longer be *your* life, but a life shared with others. It will be an ongoing, ever-unfolding spiritual experience.

The Other Shore: Serenity

∝◇◌

After the ship *Recovery* has been sailing for some time, one of the passengers suddenly shouts, "I see land!"

Following the sound of his voice, most of the friends rush to the starboard rail and peer at the horizon. Sure enough, a sliver of beach has appeared.

Slowly the boat approaches the shore. Soon the friends can make out trees and a dock, and, just beyond it, what looks like a waiting passenger train.

The ship blows its horn, and a moment later a voice booms out over the loudspeakers.

"Ladies and gentlemen, this is your captain. We're now approaching Serenity Island. In a moment I'll cut the engines and we'll begin the last part of our approach. I'll join all of you on deck shortly." A few seconds later, the boats engines stop throbbing. Gradually the boat slows until, after a few minutes, it is barely moving.

The captain—a smiling, elderly woman in a white uniform—climbs down from the wheelhouse and begins greeting passengers. As she shakes hands with Mary and Ramon, Ramon asks, "Why aren't we moving? We're still a good quarter mile from shore."

The captain nods. "This is as close as the boat can sail. From here to the shore, the water is very shallow." She gestures to a shed on the deck behind her. "In a moment my crew will hand out life rings. You'll need to swim the rest of the way."

"Swim?" Ramon asks. "I didn't expect I'd have to swim. It's been a long day and I'm tired."

The captain raises her eyebrows but maintains her smile. "Recovery is a journey, but it's not a pleasure cruise. Once you're on board, there's guidance and momentum, but you can't just kick back and become complacent."

"But I can't swim!" the young man next to Ramon says.

The captain nods again. "That's why we have life rings. Each of you will put one on, and you'll help each other get to shore."

Mary points toward the beach. "Where does the train go?" she asks the captain. "I can't quite make out its destination sign from here. Wait . . . there's an R. It says . . . it says, *Recovery.*"

"That's right," the captain says. "The journey of recovery never ends—but over time the geography changes. So sometimes the journey is by water, sometimes by land. And sometimes even by air." She points up at the sky above the island. Rising slowly into it, in the far distance, is a brightly colored passenger balloon with a large R painted on the side. In the basket beneath it, just barely visible, is a group of waving people.

"Do you think they're waving at us?" Mary asks.

"Of course," Ramon says. "And I'll bet they're shouting, 'Hey, friends! Jump in—the water's fine.'"

Acknowledgments

I need to express my deepest appreciation to Sid Farrar of Hazelden Publishing for offering me this project initially, for creatively finding solutions to challenges I faced, and especially for the utmost respect he demonstrated for me along the way.

In addition, I want to acknowledge each of the three professional writer-editors who contributed much-needed support and guidance: Doug Toft, Cynthia Orange, and especially Scott Edelstein, who helped me bring the book to completion.

And I'd like to acknowledge the thousands of men and women whose personal stories of suffering and survival have enriched my personal and professional development.

Recommended Reading

Alcoholics Anonymous, 4th Edition. New York: Alcoholics Anonymous World Services, Inc., 2001.

Twelve Steps and Twelve Traditions. New York: Alcoholics Anonymous World Services, Inc., 1981.

Drop the Rock: Removing Character Defects, 2nd Edition, by Bill P., Todd W., and Sara S. Center City, Minnesota: Hazelden Publishing, 2005. Original publication, Seattle: Glen Abbey, 1993.

A New Pair of Glasses by Chuck C. New-Look Publishing Co.: 2008.

Not-God: A History of Alcoholics Anonymous, 2nd Edition, by Ernest Kurtz. Center City, Minnesota: Hazelden Publishing, 1991.

A Program for You: A Guide to the Big Book's Design for Living, Anonymous. Center City, Minnesota: Hazelden Publishing, 1991.

As a Man Thinketh by James Allen. San Diego, CA: Dauphin, 2015. (Originally published 1903.)

The Search for Serenity and How to Achieve It by Lewis F. Presnall. Utah Alcohol Foundation, 1959.

The Sermon on the Mount: The Key to Success in Life by Emmet Fox. New York: Harper & Row, 1938, 1979.

The Twelve Steps of Alcoholics Anonymous

1. We admitted we were powerless over alcohol—that our lives had become unmanageable.

2. Came to believe that a Power greater than ourselves could restore us to sanity.

3. Made a decision to turn our will and our lives over to the care of God *as we understood him.*

4. Made a searching and fearless moral inventory of ourselves.

5. Admitted to God, to ourselves, and to another human being the exact nature of our wrongs.

6. Were entirely ready to have God remove all these defects of character.

7. Humbly asked Him to remove our shortcomings.

8. Made a list of all the persons we had harmed, and became willing to make amends to them all.

9. Made direct amends to such people whenever possible, except when to do so would injure them or others.

10. Continued to take personal inventory and when we were wrong promptly admitted it.

11. Sought through prayer and meditation to improve our conscious contract with God *as we understood Him,* praying only for knowledge of His will for us and the power to carry that out.

12. Having had a spiritual awakening as the result of these steps, we tried to carry this message to alcoholics, and to practice these principles in all our affairs.

The Twelve Steps are taken from *Alcoholics Anonymous,* 4th ed. (New York: Alcoholics Anonymous World Services, 2001), 59–60. In the same book, the "The Doctor's Opinion" and the first seven chapters provide the complete directions for the Steps as described here.

The Twelve Traditions of Alcoholics Anonymous

1. Our common welfare should come first; personal recovery depends upon A.A. unity.

2. For our group purpose there is but one ultimate authority—a living God as He may express Himself in our group conscience. Our leaders are but trusted servants; they do not govern

3. The only requirement for A.A. membership is a desire to stop drinking

4. Each group should be autonomous except in matters affecting other groups or A.A. as a whole.

5. Each group has but one primary purpose—to carry its message to the alcoholic who still suffers.

6. An A.A. group ought never endorse, finance, or lend the A.A. name to any related facility or outside enterprise, lest problems of money, property, and prestige divert us from our primary purpose.

7. Every A.A. group ought to be fully self-supporting, declining outside contributions.

8. Alcoholics Anonymous should remain forever non-professional, but our service centers may employ special workers.

9. A.A., as such, ought never be organized; but we may create service boards or committees directly responsible to those they serve.

10. Alcoholics Anonymous has no opinion on outside issues; hence the A.A. name ought never be drawn into public controversy.

11. Our public relations policy is based on attraction rather than promotion; we need always maintain personal anonymity at the level of press, radio, and films.

12. Anonymity is the spiritual foundation of all our traditions, ever reminding us to place principles before personalities. That will bring about the changes I can't.

The Twelve Traditions are taken from *Twelve Steps and Twelve Traditions* (New York: Alcoholics Anonymous World Services, 1981), 129–87.

About the Author

Fred H. has worked in the field of addiction and recovery for thirty-nine years and is the director of the retreat center for a leading addiction treatment program. He is a popular international speaker on the Big Book and the principles of the Twelve Steps.

About Hazelden Publishing

As part of the Hazelden Betty Ford Foundation, Hazelden Publishing offers both cutting-edge educational resources and inspirational books. Our print and digital works help guide individuals in treatment and recovery, and their loved ones. Professionals who work to prevent and treat addiction also turn to Hazelden Publishing for evidence-based curricula, digital content solutions, and videos for use in schools, treatment programs, correctional programs, and electronic health records systems. We also offer training for implementation of our curricula.

Through published and digital works, Hazelden Publishing extends the reach of healing and hope to individuals, families, and communities affected by addiction and related issues.

For more information about Hazelden publications,
please call **800-328-9000**
or visit us online at **hazelden.org/bookstore.**

Also of Interest

Drop the Rock, Second Edition
Removing Character Defects—Steps Six and Seven
Bill P., Todd W., and Sara S.

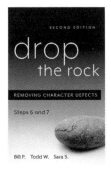

Based on the principles behind Steps Six and Seven,
Drop the Rock combines personal stories, practical
advice, and powerful insights to help readers move
forward in recovery.

Order No. 4291 ; ebook EB4291

12 Hidden Rewards of Making Amends
Finding Forgiveness and Self-Respect by Working Steps 8–10
Allen Berger, Ph.D.

Popular author and lecturer Allen Berger shares more profound recovery
insight, motivating us to earn the rewards that come with being honest
and vulnerable.

Order No. 3968; ebook EB3968

A Program for You
A Guide to the Big Book's Design for Living

Celebrating the basic text of Twelve Step recovery, this guide breathes new
life into the Big Book's timeless wisdom. Thoroughly annotated, written
with down-to-earth humor and simplicity, it offers a contemporary context
for understanding the Big Book.

Order No. 5122; ebook EB5122

For more information about Hazelden publications,
please call **800-328-9000**
or visit us online at **hazelden.org/bookstore.**